# Jenny Fensom

# *WAG TALES*

## *An Anthology of Rescued Dogs*

~~~~~~~~~~~~~~~~

**Edited and Published**
**d'Arblays Press**

This Edition first published in 2005 by

d'ARBLAYS PRESS
1 North Hall Mews
Pittville Circus Road
Cheltenham
Gloucestershire


*Printed in England*
*by*

Creeds the Printers
Broadoak
Bridport, Dorset DT6 5NL

**ISBN: 0-954-8646-1-1**


**A CIP** record for this book is available from the British Library

*In memory of*

## WIN AND JOHN

*whose lives were dedicated to the welfare of animals*

# F O R E W O R D

As a life-long owner of dogs I am delighted that Jenny has put together this delightful selection of heart-warming stories about man's best friend.

The relationship and mutual respect between dog and man has stretched back over the centuries to when man first tamed the wolf.

Over the years dogs have earned their place in history as tough and loyal workers; they have also brought joy, simple pleasure and companionship to young and old alike.

Some examples I can think of are the Polar Explorers and their Huskies, the fearless Rottweilers who fought alongside the Romans, and today's placid Guide Dogs and the trusting Police Dogs who do so much good in the fight against crime.

I was particularly touched by the story of Jackson the roaming Black Lab – I have one all of my very own who strays as much and is naughtier by far!! The story was also very relevant to me as my ancestor Stephen Coleridge fought the great anti-Vivisectionist case in the early 20th Century.

As a child I was raised on fictional stories of a rescue dog called Sammy who lived and worked with Moomin trollen in Norway. These stories told by my Father were so adventurous and full of excitement they stretched my imagination and contributed to my love and respect for our four-legged friends.

I hope that you enjoy reading this book as much as I did and I wish the Cinnamon Trust all the best with their continuing good work in the South West.

*The Hon Tania Coleridge*
*The Chanters House*
*Ottery St Mary*

# PREFACE

Dogs come in all shapes and sizes – small, large, giant, pure-bred, mongrels. But all have something in common: an unconditional loyalty and love towards their owners.

The texts gathered by Jenny Fensom are a fantastic proof of the happiness dogs bring into our lives, despite the fact that human beings do not always give this loyalty back.

Royal Canin, specialist in Health Nutrition for dogs and cats, wanted to sponsor this book because it supports our philosophy of encouraging knowledge and respect for dogs. Formulating and designing the best food for dogs is our mission, but we are part of a much wider world: the world of people sharing a passion for dogs.

Sponsoring this book is our way to show our support for all those people working for the well being of our four-legged companions and sharing the same passion.

*Axel Dubois*
*Royal Canin*
*Crown Pet Foods Ltd*

# C O N T E N T S

# INTRODUCTION

I have owned dogs since I was eight years old. My first two were miniature poodles called George and Nicky. I worked during the school holidays for a boarding kennels in the village, and on leaving school started my own dog boarding kennels which I ran for almost 30 years.

I have always been involved with pet rescue, and during the 80's and 90's helped a Luton-based charity in fund-raising and fostering unwanted dogs. Some of the dogs are featured in "Wag Tales".

It was while holidaying in Sidmouth during the last few years that I began to have the idea of compiling a book about rescued dogs. I would meet pet-owners walking in the Byes in Sidmouth, and we would exchange anecdotes about our canine companions, many of which had been rescued from various animal shelters.

So here, among others, you will meet Jackson the lovable Labrador, who one day wrecked a fish stall in the town where he lived but later went on to help the campaign for the abolition of vivisection, and was mentioned in the House of Lords; Chloé the clairvoyant boxer; Biffin the cross-collie who met Prince Charles; Nell the little sheep dog who used to run away from the sheep; Shelley the lurcher who swallowed her owner's gloves; Tina the clever cocker spaniel who saved her mistress's life; and, from earlier days, Peter the loyal mongrel who was his young owner's trusted companion during the Second World War.

I have belonged to Sidmouth Poetry Readers for three years, and several of the dog-loving members have contributed poems and anecdotes about their pets.

I hope that this book will be enjoyed by many. The proceeds from the sale will go to an animal charity.

*Jenny Fensom*

# THE GOOD COMPANIONS

*Histories are more full of examples of the fidelities of dogs than of friends.*
*Alexander Pope*

## ALICE

She tottered towards me on rickety legs, her long thin tail wagging feebly.

"You'll have a job trying to find a home for her!" the veterinary nurse exclaimed, "She must be at least fifteen."

"She's not going anywhere," I said firmly, "she's coming home with me!"

The nurses at the surgery had christened her Geraldine but I didn't think she looked like a Geraldine – no, she was definitely an Alice. If she had been a human being she would have been a Victorian parlour maid, prim and demure, wearing a lace cap and apron. She was like a loyal old family retainer who knew her place and was happy to remain there. I can always see human counterparts in all the dogs I have owned!

Alice had been found wandering the streets of Luton and taken by the police to the local vet. She was a small whippet-type breed with a suggestion of Staffordshire Bull Terrier in the lines of her head. Her muzzle and forehead were speckled grey with age and by the state of her undercarriage she had borne many a litter. She was actually in season when she was found. The few teeth she had required attention, her coat was poor, and she badly needed a bath.

In the days following she made a dramatic improvement. I gave her a bath in the old tin tub out in the garden. It was probably the only one she had ever had and as she sat there with her nose pointed upwards there was an expression of pure bliss on her ancient face as the warm soapy water sluiced over her.

I took her to the vet when she had finished her season, had her spayed and a dental op at the same time. After the operation she gained weight and a lot more confidence. She mixed in well with the other four canines in the family and her greatest joy was to join in walks, when she proved she was not too old to scent out a rabbit and give chase. Alice had regained her health, self-respect and dignity.

After a few months I decided to put her photograph in the local paper to see if anyone would claim her. I felt I had to do this in case she had wandered far off from home and there was a worried owner anxious for news of an elderly pet.

No one came forward and I concluded that she had probably belonged to an old person who had died and the heartless relatives had turned her out, abandoning her to her fate.

So Alice stayed with us and spent about three years in comfort and security: a little lady with great dignity and presence.

**Alice with Jenny**

## OSCAR (Mr Samgrass)

Several months after Alice joined the family another pathetic waif, very similar to her in appearance, arrived on the scene.

Oscar, or Mr. Samgrass as he was later nicknamed, had been taken to the same vet as Alice, as a road traffic accident case. He had been hit by a car and his leg was badly injured.

He was skin and bone, starving hungry and I judged him to be about nine years old. His coat was thin and greying, his head was like that of a small Labrador. He could run like a whippet and had all the intelligence and sensitivity of the breed. In spite of his wretched miserable condition his tail never stopped wagging from the moment I first set eyes on him until the sad day, six or seven years later, when the vet put him to sleep. I have never before or since owned a more grateful and devoted dog than Oscar.

His photograph was put in the paper but he was never claimed. A family offered to take him in but the other dogs they owned bullied him. Another lady had him for just one day: he escaped from her while tied up outside a shop and I spent the whole of one week walking the streets on the estate where she lived searching for him. We found him eventually, badly traumatized, so I took him home with me and firmly resolved to keep him. He became the devoted companion to Alice, who might well have been his mother they looked so much alike.

He adored Gemma the Yorkshire Terrier, but the two dogs he worshipped and idolized were our two Airedales, Nan and her daughter Grace. It was amusing to watch him accompanying the dignified duo at a respectful distance as they promenaded our large garden. He would trot with humble devotion behind them, tail wagging in hopeful anticipation of being noticed. My brother, who always walked Nan and Grace at the weekends or on summer evenings, would try in vain to leave the house without him but invariably after a few minuets there would be heard the thudding of paws on the path and Oscar would catch them up panting with triumph. So Anthony would bring the trio home, with Oscar's collar attached to one of the leads.

Another amusing little trick peculiar to him was that, after licking his dinner bowl clean, he would carefully place a small dainty paw right in the middle of the dish, anchoring it firmly to the floor so that not the tiniest morsel would escape his eager tongue. There were certainly no flies on Oscar!

In photographs Oscar would never be left out. While the mother and daughter would pose with regal poise on the lawn, invariably there would be Oscar's lowly little grey head preening proudly in the foreground of the picture. Oh yes, he certainly fancied his chances!

So he became known as Mr Samgrass, after the character in "Brideshead Revisited" by Evelyn Waugh. Samgrass was the name of the Oxford tutor who shadowed the aristocratic Flyte family, trying to get whatever he could out of them for his own personal ends. Of course in no way did Oscar have the same odious, devious nature as the literary character but somehow or other, because the television series was showing at the time, the name stuck and he was called Samgrass almost as often as Oscar!

I remember on one late summer evening we walked the dogs at a local beauty spot when Grace disappeared with Oscar. They vanished into the woods and despite our calling would not return. We stood for what seemed like ages shouting until we were hoarse. Eventually we decided to return home hoping to find them waiting there in the drive. They were not there, so later - at about 10.30 pm - Anthony went back to the woods with a torch and whistled and called. Still no sign of them so, miserably, we went off to bed leaving the side gate open. I did not sleep and lay awake in tears blaming myself for letting them off the lead. Grace could be very wayward and wilful at times and was not as obedient as her mother Nan. Then I heard the chink and rattle of a disc against a chain collar and the patter of paws up the side of the house. I called to Anthony and we both rushed out into the garden where on the lawn, bathed in the dappled moonlight, sat two pyramid shapes.

They were both unsure of the reception they would get but of course we were too relieved to be cross with them.

With his streetwise skill and knowledge, Oscar had brought Grace home through the woods, across the fields and the main road to safety. I know he would never have left her to fend for herself.

On another occasion he proved his devotion to Alice in likewise fashion. I was exercising the two of them in a field that adjoined the busy A6. By this time Alice was beginning to have sight problems and would become confused and disorientated at times. She must have scented a rabbit and had shot through a gap in the hedge and on to the path running along the A6. She started to head off blindly towards Luton and I began to pelt off after her. Oscar sensing the danger and my panic shot past me on the path and raced past Alice, rounding her up with all the skill of a trained sheepdog and headed her back to where I stood waiting with their leads. Extra treats for them both when we got home!

In May 1987 Oscar and Alice had a terrible ordeal when they were stolen with my car from our driveway. I had just returned home with them after an outing and had gone into the house leaving them asleep in the back of the car. I was only gone about ten minutes and when I returned to the car, to my absolute horror and disbelief, it had gone - with the two dogs still inside. It was one of the worst weekends I have ever spent. We searched everywhere; friends, neighbours and the local pet rescue groups all joined forces in the search. The police were informed and it was announced on local radio. I was becoming desperate, but early on the Monday morning I received a phone call from a police constable from a village called Sandon, near Baldock, about eighteen miles away.

The car had been used for a robbery and had been dumped at Sandon, with the two dogs inside it. The thieves had actually left the sun roof open so there was some air for the dogs. Very good of them!

**Oscar and Alice as featured in "The Daily Mail"**

# Dog-nap ordeal for Oscar and Alice

These two mongrels look relaxed now – Oscar finds life one big yawn and Alice is obviously thinking about dinner – but their owner had real cause for concern when her car was stolen with the dogs in the back.

The two former strays were snoozing on the rear seat – and they were napping again when the car was found abandoned 36 hours later. Owner Jenny Fensom said: "I wasn't a bit worried about the car, just concerned about the dogs. They were all right but a bit hungry. They really tucked into the turkey dinner I gave them."

The locals around Streatley, Bedfordshire, are familiar with the dogs from their fund-raising activities for the animal charity PAWS.

Two friends drove me over to pick them up from the police constable's house and there they stood patiently waiting for me, Oscar's tail still wagging, but dear little Alice looking shaken and confused. I always wondered afterwards why I never heard her bark again after her ordeal.

The Daily Mail got to hear of the story and came out and photographed the two dogs. Jilly Cooper, whom I had once written to in connection with a local charity I supported, sent me a charming letter, congratulating me on their safe return. Alice and Oscar celebrated their rescue with a special turkey dinner!

These two little waifs brought a lot of joy and happiness into my life; they showed me great love and devotion during the years they lived with me. Alice died after a massive stroke and we buried her under a small Christmas tree at the top of the garden. Oscar lived on for a few more years and then succumbed to heart failure and it was kindest to have him put to sleep. We laid him to rest next to his real or adopted mother and fifteen or so years later the tree stands twenty feet tall, proudly towering over all the others. I remember those two faithful creatures every time I look at it.

**Nan, Oscar (Mr Samgrass) and Grace**

# TAILS WAG

*Tis sweet to hear the watch dog's honest bark*
*Bay deep mouthed welcome as we draw home;*
*Tis sweet to know there is an eye will mark*
*Our coming, and look brighter when we come.*

*Lord Byron, from Don Juan*

## JACKSON

When I first read my friend Sheila Vanderstay's account of her late black Labrador Jackson's many adventures I was between laughter and tears. Although I'd never met him I felt that I'd always known him! Here Sheila writes in her own words.

It was a relief as, gasping for breath, I was able to stop running as I saw the large black dog coming towards me, a plastic belt round his neck, being led on a piece of thick string by a neighbour. Exhausted as I was, I was still able to summon up overwhelming feelings of dislike, bordering on hate. The dog's stomach was so bloated that it swayed from side to side as he walked. As I got nearer there came the nauseous stench of rotting fish. If someone had told me then that this dog would one day be as dear to me as breath, would own me, body, mind and spirit, I would probably have replied with a sneer.

I was regretting, for the twentieth time in three weeks, volunteering to give him a home. But the phone caller had been desperate, the three new homes they had found so far for this dog had all pronounced him unmanageable, and he had been promptly returned. "But please, he has been through hell, he just needs TLC, please, please don't send him away again." I was a soft touch for such a story.

Although I had owned many dogs, I had never had a fence jumper. Our garden was fenced all round, with netting across the end, no other dog had escaped from it. Until now. This one jumped over, scratched under, pushed through or waited craftily for someone to open it, and he would be gone, out of sight in seconds. Before long our family life had been given over to guarding him, tying him up, threatening, pleading, to little avail. He outwitted our attempts almost hourly, leaving us to phone police, or answer the door to strangers who had found him, or drop everything to rush off and collect him. It was obvious that in our house life was never going to be the same again.

On the day he was delivered to us it was Christmas Eve. We were expecting the whole family to descend for the holiday. I was frantically busy with last-minute preparations and could not give the dog much attention. I was a bit perturbed by his size - he seemed so big and black and dominant, and he moved furniture out of his way as though it was made of polystyrene. I had never owned a large dog before; our present one was a Sheltie called Willie. Our new friend was a black Labrador, taller than average, and although he seemed very large he was underweight. He had been rescued from a laboratory, and had a few wound marks on his head. In his travels, as I later discovered, he had collected worms and fleas. He had an insatiable appetite and within his first half hour with us, had stolen and eaten a cabbage and two pounds of raw pastry intended for mince pies. We were to learn that there was nothing he would not eat or steal.

So more pastry to be made, with precious minutes ticking away. When he whined to be let out for toilet, I, unaware yet of his escapist tendencies, opened the door into our large garden and let him and Willie out. Five minutes later he was gone. He had as yet no collar or tag, it was dark, he had arrived by car from twenty miles away. All Christmas preparations had to be put on hold as I roped in family and friends and neighbours to search the dark streets for this pitch black dog, whose name we did not know. But it was fruitless. We went out repeatedly and as the guests arrived they were all soon involved in the search. Christmas had got off to a bad start. We were all very tired and had all but given up. It was midnight when we heard a heavy thump on the front door, just one single thump, and there he was, unabashed, calmly expecting to be let in. He trotted past us and went to lie on the bedding as though he had lived with us all his life. How he had found his way back to us will always be a mystery. He had been with us only a few hours before running off. But happily our hours of trauma were over and we picked up the yuletide threads, but first quickly made him a makeshift collar and tag. We called him Jackson.

He soon took over our lives. All routine as we knew it vanished. The most frustrating times were mornings when, having got the family off to school and work, I would launch into the domestic round, only to be interrupted about 10 am by Jackson banging his huge body against the back door and emitting loud howls, and then wails, which got higher and higher like a soprano in full flow. He would not be quietened or ignored. So, every morning I had to drive him to the nearest green space large enough to accommodate him away from traffic. He would bound off instantly like a racehorse, until he was just a black dot in the distance. Calling him had no effect, for as yet he did not know his name. So began my jogging routine, chasing after him every morning.

We had to put locks on all the cupboards which he opened easily, pulling all the contents out in his endless search for food. He would escape from anywhere - at times ropes and even locks were useless. He was Houdini.

Now yet again today he had sneaked out, despite my best efforts as I answered the door to the postman. I phoned all the usual people and places, to no avail. Then a phone call came from a neighbour to say that she was in town and had seen a large black dog causing havoc at a fish stall. The owner was shouting and trying to catch him, helped by the customers. Jackson had found a box of fish heads which he had swallowed mostly whole, and in his chase round the stall had knocked over several boxes of fish, eating as much as he could while still evading capture. His collar with its bright new tag was missing. The fishmonger red-faced and rigid with anger, was hurling abuse and threats. My neighbour, who didn't really recognize Jackson, guessed it was him, and although she did not dare own to knowing him, offered to take him to the police station once he was captured. Then she phoned me to say come and fetch him as she had a dental appointment. I had no car that day and had to run the two miles to town to meet her. This episode, on top of all the other episodes, wearied me beyond belief; the fish made Jackson very sick and for days the house reeked, the smell was everywhere. Things had become serious.

Family discussions began in earnest as to whether we could cope for even one more day with such disruption and it was agreed that he might have to go. We would put it to the vote.

I was the only one in favour of giving it one more try, but was heavily outnumbered. I had no choice but to contact his rescuers and concede defeat. The group persuaded me to hang on a little longer, as they were at that moment engaged in a campaign, with the help of a daily newspaper, highlighting the scandal of pet stealing and they suggested that Jackson should spearhead it. The bonus being that his former owners might be traced.

We all agreed to keep him a bit longer. Shortly afterwards his photograph appeared in a local newspaper with the caption "Is this your dog?" and explaining that he was a family pet that had been stolen, and like countless others, sold for a high price to vivisection laboratories for experimentation. We could hardly contain our joy to learn that a family had recognized him and a meeting was arranged to reunite them next weekend.

By now a few more weeks had passed, and Jackson and our household had become more compatible. I had even started to look forward to the 10 am dash to open countryside, where by now Jackson was less inclined to gallop off, preferring instead to play games. I felt a vague unease at the thought of returning him to his rightful owners.

Inevitably the day dawned. A camera man and reporter from the paper amongst those waiting with the family, a thirty-something couple and their nine-year-old daughter all anxiously scanned our car as it drew up, with Jackson inside. There were tears, hugs and smiles, cameras clicked, reporters scribbled. Although Jackson recognized his family and wagged his tail and licked a lot, he kept returning to me, none of the usual lead pulling.

Then a very difficult moment for the family when the crews left and we were alone for the final parting. They confided that they had got another dog. The little girl had pined so much for Blackie, as they had called him, that they had just got to get her another pet. They had replied to the advert because they felt they just had to see him once again and to find out what had happened to him. Their house was too small for two dogs. Was there any chance of us keeping him? Of course they would quite understand if …. But I cut them short, a single tear of joy betrayed me. I hugged this great black nuisance and bundled him gratefully back into the car. I knew there would be difficult days ahead, the problems had not gone away, but from now on he was truly mine, from choice.

In the coming months Jackson became a minor celebrity. After much newspaper coverage, the British Union for the Abolition of Vivisection (BUAV) used his story in their magazine Liberator. They asked for black and white photos of him which I took. His face featured on their Stolen Pets posters and whenever they held rallies, huge pictures of Jackson were paraded, offering £500 reward for information leading to conviction of pet thieves. There were hand-out leaflets of him on street collection days. He was still referred to as Blackie, as it wasn't generally known that we were not the original owners.

He was even mentioned in The House of Lords, again as Blackie, by Lord Houghton who was an outstanding campaigner on animal issues and who used his enormous parliamentary and governmental experience to promote the campaign to stamp out pet stealing, as well as other animal rights causes. Even TV became interested and sent out a camera-man to film him. I don't know if it was ever shown, as we don't get Carlton Television in Devon.

Over the next few years life with Jackson became easier. There was a gradual deepening of our relationship with him. We had moved out of the town to a small village, to a house surrounded by farmland. Despite having two acres of garden to romp in, he would still race off, my dear black dot in the distance. Usually to return dripping with cow pats and I instantly had to drop everything to hose him down which he loved, treating it as a game. Our house was near a canal and despite the farmland and huge garden, he still demanded, with wails and door thumps, our walk every morning. We became a familiar sight as we walked down through the village, stopping at the school playground to chat to our grandchildren and their friends, who loved to pat the dogs - three now, with a Jack Russell called Tommy. The moment Jackson reached the canal path, he would hurl himself into the water, emerging covered in a curtain of green slime and water weed which he would shake all over us.

Over the fifteen years he was with us, he became a much-loved family member, more dear than any words of mine can express. There are many stories of our times together, too many to relate here. Wherever we were he was there also, with his quizzical expression, mischievous, lovable, and huge. So many memories, it was unthinkable that we must part. As he grew old and grey the dread grew. Fifteen years was nowhere near long enough, we needed eternity.

Various ailments began to beset him. Arthritis was the worst. Eventually the canal walks had to stop. Heartbreaking it was to have to face his hurt and disbelief as I set off without him each morning with Tommy and Kip, another Jack Russell. Eventually his legs began to give way and we knew that the end was near. Who *does* know when the time is right. Are we ever ready to say goodbye?

Then at Christmas, fifteen years to the day of his arrival, he could not stand without falling. I called the vet to our house, knowing what the verdict would be.

Keeping our goodbyes as dignified as such a moment would allow, I held his dear face in my hands as he quietly left us. No need to describe the heartbreak. Any dog lover will know it. I had lost precious dogs before. But in every dog-lover's life one shines out, I think, above the rest. One special soul mate. We were, to quote Aristotle, "a single soul dwelling in two bodies".

I could not quieten the raw grief at his loss, the empty silence after his body was gone. The realization that this time next week, next month, next year, Jackson would still be dead. What a price we pay for our loves. Two hours after he had gone I started to write to him. I wrote every day for two weeks, recalling memories, telling him how I felt. This helped to assuage the initial grief. He had been such a huge part of my life, unbearable that he had gone somewhere without me, would never return with his familiar thump on the door. Not even in my dreams.

It was eighteen months before I felt comfortable rather than sad with my memories. I was then able to bring another black Labrador into my life. His name is Harry. He is love, laughter and pure delight. Since this is a breed I would probably never have known, I will always consider Harry as a beautiful gift from Jackson.

**Jackson**

## CHLOÉ

Chloé has every reason to wag that lovely, long liberated tail as she makes her way around Sidmouth with her master and mistress every day.

Anne Everest-Phillips, in her own words, tells Chloé's story.

Chloé - The Camouflage Dog.

"Please, just do me a favour and take her home on appro for the weekend and see if you can persuade her to eat," begged the kindly owner of the Boxer rescue centre.

We looked at the ungainly bag of bones lying in the corner of the field. The head lifted, the patchwork face turned upwards with the largest lugubrious eyes we had ever seen in a dog. Those eyes told us all we needed to know; here was unconditional love if only we'd accept the emaciated form, every vertebra so easily counted down the spine, the spindly legs and *that tail.*

"Back street bred I'm afraid. Far too much white on her and as for that *tail…*"

Tails were definitely not in vogue for boxers. Not ill treated though, just pining for the family from whom she had been so abruptly severed. The young man had been tearful as he had handed her over, turned on his heel and walked briskly away. Few facts were established – she was about two and a half years old, would need re-vaccinating in July … and her name…Was it Cleo or Chloé?

As my husband gently lifted her on to the back seat of the car, I asked her directly, "Are you Chloé?". Yes, there was the feeble wave of the long tapering tail and so that was settled. Where had we seen those eyes before, that expression? She sat bolt upright in the corner of the seat and started to show an interest in what was happening. An adventure? But just what kind of adventure? We could feel those eyes boring into the back of our heads as we sped towards Sidmouth. The car slowed and approached our house and we opened the rear door. "Lifted down? No thank you, I can manage," and the emaciated creature cast an eye round the garden, up the steps, into the hall and down the passage into the kitchen. "A new rug on the floor? That'll suit me fine." The legs gave way and Chloé found her new home.

"Yes thank you, I might just be tempted." The eyes were cast critically over the proffered bowl of food. She lumbered up, and stared, sniffed, and peered again. We waited with bated breath, and then success, those great jaws opened and she started to eat.

Each room was inspected and seemed to meet with tacit approval, then back to the kitchen and bed. The three of us spent a quiet, happy evening together. From the dog basket came contented breathing and the still expressive eyes almost closed, but not quite. We were obviously being summed up. Eventually it was bedtime, still not a sound. The eyes opened wide with alarm as we each bade her goodnight. Reluctantly, we closed the door and started for the stairs. A sudden piercing howling started and continued. In turn we sat with Chloé but she would not stop until we were both with her. If one of us disappeared the howling started again, reaching a crescendo which did not stop until all three of us were together again. Eventually, and much against our firmly held views, as we had never allowed a dog to sleep upstairs, we took Chloé and her bed up with us. Then there was no sound except almost inaudible breathing and a faint regular thrumming of a happy tail until the alarm clock rang.

Chloé had started to lay down the ground rules. She had decided to come and live à trois and a threesome we must henceforth remain. For a good six weeks Chloé would not allow us to separate. If one of us peeled off to go in a shop she refused to move until we were all present and correct and then her tail would wag so violently that it posed a danger to any innocent passerby.

A new pantomime had come to Sidmouth. Oblivious of all public opinion Chloé knew how to count to three. We realized just how disturbed she had been at being abandoned and we started to piece together something of her previous life. There had been a red car and children.

Dogs are said to be colour blind, but every red car in town had to be inspected and if it contained children there was eager anticipation and then the inevitable disappointment.

It took a long time before we could pass a red car or a family group with children without closer inspection.

Chloé's world gradually widened and we realized where we had seen those eyes before. Yes, Gromit from" Wallace and Gromit". We could read the expression, "Well, this is life and I'd better make the most of it!" This expression, part martyr part cynic, gets her everywhere. In the Prospect Newsagents - a biscuit? "I don't mind if I do. Thanks. I'll be back tomorrow." Quite shameless. So the habit of being spoiled rotten started. "Oh, yes, that kindly apple-cheeked lady serving vegetables is offering me a lovely fishy treat". Hesitation, then, friends for life. *This* is the life! Friend Carol can be relied on for a Saturday treat. The strange thing, however, is that there seems to be an inordinate number of Saturdays in Carol's weeks.

Sidmouth too, seems to be to Chloé's liking. The beach, well, that's of interest only on sandy days when she enjoys nothing better than burying a treasured pebble and then digging it out wildly. Perhaps one day she will meet the dingo cousins coming from the opposite direction. Peak Hill and Knowle have rabbits but chasing is only half hearted - just what does one do with one if it is caught? One day a rabbit was a little tardy and there was a confrontation between Chloé and Peter Rabbit. They stared at one another. We eased the big paws apart and off ran Peter to give to the warren an exaggerated account of the event.

Doggy Heaven is the Byes. Here the grass stretches for miles, there are trees to sniff and hide under, dozens of chums to play hide and seek with and then there is The Sid. There is nothing, but nothing, that a landlubber dog, who is privately a little scared of the sea, with its unpredictable waves, likes more than messing about in slowly-running, shiny water. There are even bold ducks to exchange rude jokes. Then the joy of slithering up the bank, firmly embedding thick slimy earth in one's paws before joining the family in the sunshine. What else can a dog need? Oh, yes a ball! Over there are some friendly lads playing a funny game with a ball and pieces of wood. Oh, come on Chloé, we know you can leap and catch a ball five feet from the ground but you haven't actually been *invited to join the team.* As she gets older she may still be interested in ball games, but has to realize that, like other local denizens, it is our turn to become spectators.

She still regards any visitor, postman or workman as having arrived purely for her benefit and each is greeted with a ball or a toy. Our granddaughters, aged 9 and 5, consider Chloé as the prime reason for visiting Sidmouth. Chloé allows herself to be proudly paraded through the street by a child who weighs less than she does. She enjoys the progress, graciously surveying her vassals and accepting the many compliments as her due. Does she realize that she has won the title "The Oddest Looking Pooch in Town"?

Chloé, the otherwise friendly giant, so colourfully described as the camouflage dog by a perceptive small boy, follows the Rudyard Kipling dictum that all proper dogs shall chase cats up trees. There is only one other dog in Sidmouth with whom she cannot exchange friendly greetings. Strangely it is the other Boxer named Chloé and with a tail: the feeling is mutual - so much so that either dog will bark at the other's owners even if the other Chloé is not present! Is it that each recognizes that the other is equipped with the same fashion accessory – an elegant tail? Is it the equivalent of HM the Queen and Mrs Thatcher meeting and realizing that they are wearing identical outfits? We can only guess.

She is a generous host and welcomes visiting dogs with pleasure. She even acts like a protecting East End "Minder" if young Alfie, the little Cocker Spaniel, is ever "bad mouthed" by any impertinent larger dog on the Byes.

Her taste in music runs to timpani and percussion. It is surprising what an extensive repertoire of scales and rhythms emanates from an ordinary water-filled radiator when struck excitedly by a solid tapering tail.

At home Chloé loves lazing in the garden, watching seagulls wheeling overhead or humans snipping and pruning. Indoors, she lies like the legendary Bristolian always sleeping with one eye open, anticipating footsteps or the bell. For all her rumbustiousness at greeting human callers, there are sometimes strangely calm occasions when she seems to encounter our house's friendly spirit. We notice, with some awe, how civilly she steps aside - it seems, to allow him to pass on the stairs or in rooms and corridors. She is also occasionally to be found sitting by what we can only presume is the foot of his armchair and staring fixedly into his face as he talks kindly to her or shows her his pet raven.

Dear little bag of bones lying in the corner of that field five years ago, what pleasure you have given so many. Long may you give us a firm pull on the leash to indicate which way you would like our walk to lead. Is it the Byes, the beach, or up Hillside to your special friend today? We know we shall enjoy your company in whichever way you decide, Chloé.

**Chloé with Carol Singleton**

# MONTY

## The Master's and Mistress's Story

We went to see Monty (Rocky as he then was) at his foster home in Seaton in February 2001 and fell in love with him straight away. He even offered his knuckle bone to us!

Monty was quite thin when we got him. Although Lurchers normally have a tapered look, he was underweight, so we carried on the good work of the foster home and built him up gradually.

We were extremely lucky with him considering that he had never had a collar and lead on, been in a car or house or socially trained. He was brilliant, no real problems at all. He has a wonderful temperament and a great character. He is quite a cartoon dog with a sense of humour, non aggressive and intelligent - he loves people, especially children.

He can turn a deaf ear when he is chasing pheasants. He likes socializing and showing off, and doing his party pieces - which are various tricks for any audience and, of course, for a treat.

He is well known in our local pub, where he receives lots of attention from other dog lovers. He likes his comforts and his cuddly toys, which he carries around with him one at a time.

In the evenings he loves to curl up on the sofa between his master and mistress, and who was it who once said dogs should not be allowed on furniture … it certainly is a dog's life!

So Monty has changed our lives forever and is a great joy to us. We have never owned a dog before and I don't think we could take another one, as he is our ultimate canine friend.

## MONTY'S STORY

Whoofy greetings. My name is Monty. I am a Springer Spaniel cross Lurcher, and I will be four years old in May 2004.

My story starts on a farm near Honiton, East Devon. According to the humans who rescued me I spent most of my time finding scraps in a farmyard with my dad. I was a pup of eight months and I don't remember that much. One day a carpenter came to the farm to do some work, and I overheard him "human talking" to my master at the time. He said that I looked a lovely pup - and then my master said that he had intended to train me to hunt, but did not have the time, so would probably have to shoot me.

Of course I did not know what this meant at the time, being a dog, but the nice carpenter did.

He said to the farmer "If you mean that, I will take him home with me today." Which he did - I'd never been in a car before. The carpenter could not keep me but he knew of a rescue place centre, but there were no facilities for keeping dogs.

I did not do well in kennels at eight months old: it was very scary. I barked a lot because I was frightened, but then I was found a lovely foster home with some nice people in Seaton …but not for long though.

My new Master and Mistress came to see me and it was love at first sight, I even dropped my knuckle bone on my new master's toe to show them how much I liked them.

I will soon be four years old and my life has changed so much. I live in a farmhouse with fields all around and there is access to woods nearby. I chase "pheasies" (pheasants), go for long walks and have plenty of good food. I play with my master and mistress a lot: I have a house-mate called Bobo, he's a cat, but he's not so bad as cats go.

I also have lots of favourite toys with names like … Toysey, Piglet, Piggy and Dicky. And that's my story so far – so, 'lickies' goodbye!

**Monty**

## REX

Gwen Porteous used to live in Sidmouth and then moved to Swaffham in Norfolk. However, she still keeps in touch with the town by receiving the Sidmouth Herald every week. She saw my letter requesting stories of rescued pets in the East Devon area and kindly wrote to me about her late faithful Cocker Spaniel Rex.

Gwen writes:

"I had just said goodbye to my much loved Cocker Spaniel Sapphire, so I asked the lady who ran the local rescue kennels if there were any spaniels needing a good home.

She asked what breed I had had, and when I told her a Cocker Spaniel she said she knew of a Blue Roan wanting a home, so she delivered Rex the same day! It was 1994 and I was living at Lark Rise, Newton Poppleford at the time.

I don't know much about his history; only that he was four years old and had been collected from a petrol station at Okehampton.

He was kept in the rescue kennels for three weeks where his poor infected ears were treated before he was re-homed.

**Rex**

He settled down well and gave us a lot of pleasure for eight years. Alas, we had to part with him about two years ago as he became very ill and the vet could do nothing more for him. To save him further suffering we had to make the decision to let him go.

He is still missed dreadfully. Rex was such a character and so full of mischief: above is a photograph of him when he first came to us.

## SHELLEY

Lucky Shelley has lived for nine years with Anne and Beryl Frost from Sidbury.

Anne writes:

Shelley, our nine year old Lurcher, was taken to a local rescue centre at the age of about eight weeks. We had had to have our beloved Cavalier Spaniel put to sleep about three weeks earlier, after fourteen years.

**Shelley**

We enquired at the rescue centre if they had any Lurchers needing a home as we had seen one living in Sidbury and they seemed such a lovely quiet breed. After another two weeks we were told that a puppy had been rescued from travellers in Exeter. We went to see whether the pup would be our new companion and fell in love with the little darling and took her home.

She quickly became very important to my sister and me, was very clean, and when taken for walks soon learned to return to us if she ever followed another dog. Her naughty antics would fill a book. While under a year she would swallow items whole - which fortunately were always soft!

Her first lapse was when she swallowed a handkerchief from a pile of washing. The vet put a large lump of soda down her throat, we stood back and waited, true enough it *was* some washing, but it was a pair of summer silk gloves! The vet said that if any one told her their dog could not swallow tablets then she would say she knew one that could swallow gloves! Shelley has now stuck to swallowing food, which is a blessing!

In all she is a lovely, intelligent companion, loves chasing and retrieving a ball, is very good with other dogs on her walks and to those who visit her home or join her in the car. She is rather given to barking when people come and this is sometimes a problem. Nevertheless, we love her dearly and are always grateful that she came to us.

## BERTIE

Writer P D Pemberton lives in Sidmouth and has owned a variety of rescued dogs over the years. The following amusing dog tale is about a rescued dog named Bertie (pseudonym) who belonged to a neighbour.

Bertie was totally terrier. In his winter wool however he didn't look it. Instead of the sharp, square jaw all you could see was a rounded mass. The mass resembled a woolly–animal pyjama case – or a rug with thick pile that needed mowing.

Very old and very young ladies saw him as a desirable teddy bear; and did not immediately notice the keen, dark eyes peering through the wool. The keen, dark eyes were watching for a sudden movement such as that of a bird or a foot that could be seized and worried by the sharp teeth. The ladies old and young alike realized their mistake too late and yelped like puppies as their feet were attacked.

He was found abandoned in a park when he was about two. His new owner couldn't understand how anyone could desert such a lively, eager friendly young dog. Then when Bertie had got his breath back and had set out to be a terrier, he started ravaging clothes lines and visitors' moving feet. Relations, milkman and the paper boy learned to move exceptionally fast. (His owner always donned Wellington boots before going downstairs in the morning). She had to give up the postman. Bertie probably viewed letters flipping through his letter box as dangerous missiles, like IRA letter bombs. It was obviously his duty to destroy these. He tormented and shredded them. The letter box, too, had to be sealed. A notice was put on it directing letters to be delivered to a neighbour's house.

During our first summer as a neighbour, our sunny, garden days were punctuated by the shrill cries of his owner as she pounded down her garden in full cry after Bertie and the tea towel, socks or knitting wool.

"No, Bertie. No! NO! NO! NO!" Her voice would go up the scale, arriving at top doh before she reached the end of the garden. After the first GRRR was heard through the hedge we could guess the timing of each ascending "NO!" We were tempted to join in the chorus.

After several GRRRS and shrieks there would be a sudden silence. Had Mrs Bertie, as we called her, lost control and throttled him? We wondered the first time. No. The silence simply meant that she had cornered him among the cabbages and was struggling to remove the rags from his mouth. It was good, vigorous exercise for a woman in her fifties, but hardly worth rescuing whatever it had been, unless she had managed an unusually quick sprint.

When spring came and windows opened, some listened for the cuckoo. *We* listened for the "No no NO's!" heralding the opening of Mrs Bertie's steeplechase season. On some summer days the entertainment was of a high standard, as she fought energetically to regain control of the garden hose. Other screams – short, sharp ones of shock - meant something different to the discerning ear.

"That's the dustbin again", said my husband with the triumphant smile of a doctor sure of his diagnosis.

Bertie's technique with a dustbin was to charge as a tank in battle, nudge it over sideways and then push the lid off with his nose. Mrs Bertie took to keeping bricks on the top to prevent him from reaching dangerous, splintering bones.

After all she did love him. And his unselective crunching of the bin's contents usually made him sick. But neighbours' dustbins were caught unaware when Bertie managed to escape from home. On those days you could tell which way he was travelling by the trails of rubbish-strewn gardens.

When he was still young, and Mrs Bertie busy, we used to take him out with our two bitches in the car and drive him to fields where he could run free. There was little time to train him. We concentrated on exhausting him and, regularly, on separating him from Emma. Spayed bitches don't fight. Dogs don't fight bitches. Well, on every outing, sooner or later Bertie and his little teeth would go after Thisbe's back legs. Sometimes he would butt her hindquarters off the ground with his head. This was too rough for the more graceful Thisbe. When cornered, she cowered motionless in long grass. Emma had to hurry across and snap at Bertie. He snapped and lunged in reply. We always had to separate them in the scuffle. We asked a Dog Trainer's advice about this.

"Never come across a dog fighting a bitch" he said disbelievingly. Then, at our feet, Bertie came back at Emma for Round Two.

"See what you mean," said the trainer, moving his feet back out of the arena and leaving us to separate them.

In parks, we were obliged to seek empty patches, avoiding large dogs and children with shoes and feet they didn't want detached. So we took him to a dog training class while his owner was ill. We had usually been able to appease him with gentleness when he seized our hands or gloves. We'd let the prey go limp, like a dead rat. Bertie would lose interest in the sport. He would stand on his short stubby legs and lick us, inviting us to rub his chest.

In training classes however he had to submit to firmer discipline. A choke chain was applied to stop him from nipping other paws as they passed.

When it was his turn to go Down! – full length on the floor - he was busy looking round for targets. So, as instructed, we pushed him firmly down. Taken by surprise, he twisted round and snarled at the hand on his back. The training hall was full of the sound of Bertie ready for the kill. "Nonsense!" I shouted, soothing his back with the hand at risk. He relaxed and relented, muttering.

The trainers laughed. "Has he drawn blood yet?"

I explained that he wasn't really vicious, just determined and affectionate in his own rough way. He came to heel and Sat in a collected model fashion, peering upwards through the fur in case there was a reward in hand.

If called when he wanted to investigate another dog in a distant corner of the hall, then of course he didn't come. He'd shoot across the hall with his peculiar rocking-horse movement and great velocity. The highly polished floor making him skid and overshoot his target, bouncing into the wall.

Other dog owners laughed.

"You have to be careful" warned the trainer. "Bright dogs soon learn how to make you laugh. Then they know they can get away with murder." Murder being a word Mrs Bertie didn't care to think about, she started a course of private lessons with a trainer.

Heroically, she resisted the temptation to let him loose; and for months walked him long distances on the lead until control had been largely established. He could now be commanded with fair success, but Mrs Bertie chose quiet spots to release him.

At home, visiting friends with target feet still had to rise slowly and carefully from chairs. Running grandchildren were at risk unless Bertie was tied up. To compensate for being attached to a line in the garden when the window cleaner came, Bertie, when loose, concentrated his considerable energies on escaping.

For many months he battled and bludgeoned his way over a five foot fence, a horticultural and regretful neighbour's garden and up, over, and down our assorted defences of fencing, trees and dense bushes. His aim when bored was to visit our two bitches. They would patently rather have waited until he had lost all his teeth. They were unwilling to sunbathe in their own garden unless we were present to protect them.

Indoors we all leapt up if Thisbe barked her distinctive warning; "Bertie, the woolly peril". As he crashed through undergrowth or actually down a tree trunk into our garden, she was the first to hear the jingling of his metal disc. A dropped bunch of keys, making the same sound in the house, caused panic and retreat.

Normally, a rapid closing of the French window and yard gate, with its barricades, restricted Bertie to our garden. When Emma and Thisbe were safely on furniture above the Bertie-line we used to go in the garden and attach a lead to the resigned Bertie. We then whisked him through our house and along the road to his home. He trotted demurely to heel.

AUNTIE

Mais vous allez revenir ?

- as long as you're coming back ?

*Copyright © P D Pemberton*

*By permission of P D Pemberton*

After we had taken in a Retriever dog, Jeeves, to join Emma and Thisbe, life became more acute. Bertie was outraged, incensed by the presence of this usurper to his rights. Both the dog trainers and the local vet were convinced that Bertie was out to kill Jeeves, who also shared this view. Bertie redoubled his efforts to escape. We now needed a Berlin Wall.

Jingle some keys and now Jeeves jumped sideways like the rest of us … with good reason!  TAIL PIECE - The solution to the problem? We moved house.

## TINA

Miss Frida Harris of Gloucestershire has a lot for which to thank her loyal little Cocker Spaniel Tina, when one day she saved her mistress's life.

Here is the story in Frida's own words.

My spaniel was a very ordinary dog until one day when she became a life saver. We'd both been swimming – the sea was grand – not even terribly rough or cold and the two of us, always good companions, were chasing a ball. Life was good. Tina was splendid. Suddenly life was NOT GOOD - I fell over my own feet, (have you ever done that?) and the pain in my left arm was excruciating. I don't think I'd ever known the meaning of that word before.

I was only in my swim suit and shivering violently. I had no power to draw on my clothes. They seemed to be glaring at me in scorn or disbelief. Tina was my only hope. I think she'd already sensed the serious nature of my fall. Not a single person was in sight. It was always early morning when I swam.
"Tina," I pleaded "fetch somebody!" I prayed hard and managed to put Tina's lead on, but it was agony.

Did she understand? She was a five-year-old blue roan Cocker Spaniel and this would test her. But she ran off, lead flapping, up the cliff side.

I had to drag my clothes round my shivering body. It seemed ages, though I think it wasn't long, then, here was Tina with a young man clutching her lead, my deliverer. He looked scared stiff. I suppose a naked woman, shaking and obviously freezing did present a challenge. What could he do? He wasn't much more than a school boy. But surely they taught First Aid at school?

So my first comforting words were for him and at last, with some difficulty, I was almost respectably covered. Then I was in command of the situation. After all I was the teacher wasn't I? He was just a young scared lad.

"Now look," I admonished him through still chattering teeth, "you take Tina and go to the cliff top and, at the Ice Cream Shop, ask them to phone the people next door". I gave him the number, which I remembered.

"Tell them what's happened. Perhaps Tina could stay there till I get to the top. I'm going to try and drag myself that far."

The lad looked relieved, he wasn't much more than a boy, fifth- or sixth-former perhaps. "I'll keep Tina with me if you like" he said. "She likes me. I only live near the shop."

True enough Tina seemed to have transferred her affection to the lad, so my only concern was for myself.

I was in agony, but very slowly edged my way up the cliff. My mouth was totally dry and the few early blackberries, though unripe, actually did help a bit. The boy - I'd already decided to give him a big reward - was still near the shop, clutching Tina. I was glad to see he'd bought himself a large ice cream!

"They're coming as soon as they're dressed," the boy assured me as he handed over Tina's lead. The dog looked suitably pleased to see me but still pulled towards the boy with his ice!

"I think I'd better stay with her till they come" he said "lovely dog". He patted Tina's head. "She really saved your life."
"So did you," I told the lad who looked embarrassed now the emergency was over. "I'll be thanking you properly later on."

The rest of the day passed like a dream (or more like a nightmare really). My friendly driver was kind and drove me to the Emergency Wing of the hospital, where they informed me I had broken my collar bone and strapped me up.

When all the excitement was over, I spent long hours just sitting and hugging Tina. I couldn't very well hug my deliverer, whose name was Ralph. Apparently he'd only recently lost his retriever and Tina was almost a godsend to him.

I'd known Golden Retrievers and that they

**Tina with Frida Harris**

could be trained to save lives, but Tina was a lovely ordinary blue roan Cocker Spaniel, which just shows!

Tina was a rescue dog.

## BEN

Gillian Sexton from Tipton St John writes about her rescue dog Ben.

My husband and I bought Ben from the Blue Cross Centre at Tiverton in October 2003 after having lost our previous rescue dog Bazil the previous August. He is a three-year-old Border Collie Cross. He had been living on a small-holding with a very dominant female dog who bullied him, ate his food and generally gave him a hard time, leaving him timid and lacking confidence. He had never been socialized and was therefore afraid of other dogs and people.

Poor Ben had never played with toys or been bathed and groomed. Within a month he had learned how to chase after toys thrown for him and loves playing in the garden, followed by his daily groom! He is still worried by people but we are getting there slowly. We have the help of an animal behaviourist organized by the Blue Cross and his advice has been invaluable.

**Ben**

## NORMAN AND SNOOPY

Di Hern of Liverton has adopted two adorable terriers called Norman and Snoopy.

I phoned the local rescue centre when we had to have our small black and tan terrier bitch put to sleep. Ideally we wanted another small terrier but the assistant at the centre said there were only big dogs available. Then she checked the files and found there was a small wire haired Jack Russell dog still living with its owners, eleven months old, good with cats and children, called Norman.

The owners wanted to vet possible new owners, which was why Norman was not at the centre.

They owned a small hotel and a lively character like him did not mix well with the more prim and proper of the guests staying there. So it was a choice between the dog or their livelihood.

To say Norman was hyperactive was an understatement. When he arrived he was like a whirlwind. He took the logs from the fire and chewed them all up over the sitting room floor; he chased the cat and jumped over the furniture! When we explained to his Mum and Dad that he would have to go to work with my husband who was a forester, then they agreed to let us adopt him. The baggage he brought with him was incredible! Dog beds, cushions, blankets, brushes and combs, chews, leads - in fact enough to fill a shop.

His former owners left in tears and when we went back inside we found Norman had wet on the floor and left a parcel under the table. Naughty Norman had arrived!

Once, when my husband was working in Haldon Woods, Norman decided to follow the scent of a deer across the busy express way! Thankfully a kind lady risked life and death to rescue him and phoned us to collect him. We arrived and there was Norman sitting on her knee, after having covered The Good Samaritan in mud, looking as if butter wouldn't melt!

After we had Norman a few months we returned to the rescue centre to find him a friend. We found Snoopy, a smooth Jack Russell with a long tail: all she had was a collar, no lead, no basket or toys, nothing.

To own two dogs is a real joy. They spend hours playing. Snoopy hides under an old blanket and Norman sits on her and bites her through it. The old cat is now 18 but all three have fun ambushing each other in the shrubbery. Snoopy

**Snoopy and Norman with owner Di**

goes to the woods every day with my son. My husband now drives a lorry but Norman always rides alongside him with his "NORMAN" nameplate in the window.

Our two rescue dogs have brought us so much happiness. We have no knowledge of Snoopy's past but I shall be eternally grateful to Norman's Mum and Dad in allowing us to look after the little dog they had grown to love and cherish.

## SCOOBY AND BARNEY

Scooby and Barney live with the Faulkner family in Sidmouth and the two dogs complement each other.

Mrs R Faulkner writes about her two rescued pets.

Scooby was called Scruffy when we got him, but he was much too handsome so we changed his name to Scooby when he came to live with us in April 2000. He was an 18-month-old short haired collie cross. Barney arrived a little later in the same year.

At first Scooby seemed to be rather scatty and silly but he has since proved to be extremely clever! He used to be very nervous and an escape artist, but with lots of regular long walks and a good routine he has turned into a lovable, loyal family pet with a great character. He has his own sofa where he loves to recline with his legs in the air, relaxing!

He is so good natured he allows the children to dress him up in fancy dress; he loves being groomed but hates the bath. Scooby just loves to be the centre of attention.

Barney was a stray and in poor condition when he arrived. He is a long haired collie and was about 10 years old. He is a very intelligent old boy, will walk to heel and is incredibly clever. He tries to play darts with us and has been banned from pubs if there is a match going on! He seeks approval and needs something to do all the time, always waiting for the next game of ball. We don't think he realizes he is getting on a bit.

**Barney**

Both dogs are good friends and their characters rub off on one another, probably because of Barney's mature wisdom and Scooby's learning from him. They are like brothers and have a great time running on the beach and in the woods together. They give us much pleasure and make us laugh every day.

**Scooby**

## PETER

Norma Fulwood relates the story of Peter, her faithful mongrel companion who grew up with her during the Second World War, after Norma and her parents had moved away from Birmingham to live in the country.

Before we left Birmingham Dad and I went to Barnes Hill RSPCA Kennels, where we met Peter for the first time. He was a medium-sized mongrel and had been left shut up all day in a garage while his owners were at work

After a few days with our family Peter became ill and a friend who knew about dogs told us to give him Aspirin and to keep him indoors. But Peter insisted on going out when he needed to, so we tried to wrap him up in one of Dad's old jackets. But independent Peter soon decided he was having none of that and got himself out of the wrappings and then went out! He would only allow Mum to wait outside with him, patiently waiting for her to light the torch even if there was a moon shining. One night Mum was ill and Dad had to do the honours.

After a few days, Dad said that Peter had had enough Aspirin. He could hardly stand up, let alone walk, so we then gave him lacto–something tablets, again on our friend's advice. And after that Peter recovered - from distemper.

Then we moved to Bittel Lane. The day we moved was very foggy. In fact one of the removal men had to walk in front of the van, as visibility was almost nil. In the evening we took Peter down the lane for a walk on the lead and if it had not been for him leading us back to our garden gate we'd still be walking!

We did not want Peter to wander on his own in the surrounding countryside and fields, nor did we wish to chain him up. Dad built him an enclosure leading from the kitchen and with a gate into the back garden. There was a large area for him to run around in, and from the chestnut fencing Peter had a good view of the back garden and surrounding fields, the drive and the lane. Thus he was able to greet people coming, with either joyous barks or, if appropriate, ferocious growls.

Our garden had been neglected. The house had been commandeered by Service personnel, but there were some beautiful plum and pear trees. As there were no apple trees, Dad bought some Bramley and Ellison Orange bushes.

We also kept poultry and Dad built another enclosure for them with a good wooden hen house. We went to Birmingham Market and bought a dozen day-old chicks, most of which we were able to rear. Mum bought some more birds from Avonmouth College and some beautiful ducks from Studley Cottage. These were much admired and were almost as big as geese! Aunty Blanche, who kept a poultry farm, also gave us some Light Sussex, Rhode Island Reds and North Holland Blues.

Besides the role of house guardian, Peter also assumed the duty of poultry supervisor, as well as being senior family pet and in charge of two cats.

One day Peter came into the kitchen and yelped urgently to us to follow him. When we got round to the poultry enclosure there was one of the hens, Maggie, hanging upside down on the wire, she'd caught her foot in the netting while trying to climb it.

It was amazing that Peter had alerted us, as the part of the fence where Maggie was trapped was not visible from Peter's enclosure. Another time he led us to where one of the cats was caught in the hawthorn hedge, again out of sight of his line of vision. Could these be two examples of inter-species communication?

One February while shopping at a department store in town I bought a load of dress material. It was a very heavy load to carry to the bus depot but I managed to get it there, feeling a sense of euphoria at my lucky purchase. On the way home I suddenly realized that I had to carry the whole lot up the lane to the house. However would I manage it? So over the air I sent a mental message to Peter - "Peter, tell them to meet me. PLEASE!" I alighted from the bus and then saw the beam of a torch waving, and there was Mum and Peter. Mum told me that, despite being sent back to his chosen resting place under the table, he had repeatedly walked over to her, laid his chin on her knee and looked into her eyes. "He wants me to go and meet Norma, and I'm going!" she said to Dad.

We also had two cats in the family. Mum was a Commandant in the British Red Cross. She was phoned by Sir Peter Innes to give a course of lectures to some young people in Rubery. One day a student gave her a little black kitten which had been abandoned – the student's father had told her to take it to Mrs Fulwood, who had just lost her cat.

Mum brought him home in the car where, after entering the house, he ate a good meal before settling down for a wash. Peter approached and had a good sniff. Blackie just turned and gave him a smart tap on the nose, and then resumed his toilette. Peter's enquiring interest turned to amazement for a second. Amusement lasted longer and presaged a deep, lasting trust and friendship. The two would play together and ambush each other in the garden.

Mickey, our other cat, was very refined with marmalade markings, a white under-carriage, and long and sleek in shape. He had quite a different character to Blackie. He literally fell out of the upstairs window of the RSPCA clinic in Bristol. Dad picked him up and took him back in. The comment was "He's always doing that", so Dad brought him home.

Thus it was that both he and Blackie took up residence with us on the same day. They met on the morrow, after having spent the night in separate rooms. They were not really friends but did not fight, nor did they fraternize, to our knowledge. But when they left the house on their respective patrols, they left together. One's business commitments demanded a left turn at the back door, while the other turned right. They always returned together from opposite direction, but not necessarily from the one in which they set out. Was this a subterfuge or did they really have separate interests?

Peter usually slept in the kitchen at night on the cushioned wooden chair. Blackie would sleep on top of him so he had a warm under-blanket and Peter a warm over-blanket! The kitchen was heated by a Rayburn stove. Mickey would sleep in an arm-chair in the living room, with the connecting door open.

Peter was a marvellous guard dog and Mum and Dad were never worried about me going out alone as long as he was with me. On Sunday mornings after he had had a good brushing we would go for a long walk, sometimes through Barnt Green along the canal path or we would wander round the Lickey Hills. Animal and person respected Peter dog, and even the farm dogs took the precaution of making a detour if they saw us approaching! On our return one morning a local notorious person threatened him with a rolled up newspaper. Good old Peter jumped up at it and ripped it straight down the centre!

**Peter**

In my mind's eye is Peter eating some raw sausages, one paw on them, and looking up at us with delight on his face. They had been put down on the kitchen table, but they were his favourite food … being wartime food was rationed, so all of us shared – Mum, Dad, Peter, Mickey, Blackie and me – except of course those sausages! All good Peter things come to an end, however, and our consolation was that Peter had enjoyed living in the country and we had had the very great pleasure of his company.

## NIPPER THE VEGETARIAN DOG

Norma also has this story to relate about a little Jack Russell Terrier she and her mother once owned.

"You'll have to get either a dog or cat for company for your mother".

These words were spoken by the vet when Tussaphat katte had died.

"You're at work all day and she can't get out to meet people. Besides, living where you do you'll be soon over run by mice if you don't do something about it!"

It was all true!

We'd moved to the outskirts of a village where we knew nobody. Mum's replacement hip joint dictated our removal, and the price of bungalows our location.

"I'll get the RSPCA Inspector to find a dog for her. I know she'd prefer a dog to a cat.  We'll find her one she can be happy with."

Within a few days the Inspector carrying a cat basket, arrived. He came into the kitchen and, after unfastening the lid, lifted out a small Jack Russell and put her on the floor. "Well, what do you think to her?" Her hind legs gave way. I leapt forward. "The poor little thing!" The little black and white terrier had found a home. He told us that just over a week ago a lady had phoned and reported the sound of a dog's continuous crying. The inspector went there and found the little thing crouched at the back of the coal shed. She was completely black and the only indication of her presence was the shining of her eyes in the light of his torch.

After shutting her in his van, he reported to the lady that he had collected the dog. She escaped from the van when he went back to open the door, he chased after her and she nipped his hand as he caught her. Thus her name - Nipper!

The vet pronounced she was fit apart from two broken bones. He then vaccinated her before her admission to kennels for the night. The next day she was bathed and a beautiful white collar and white paws were revealed, together with brindled legs.

We were warned about her limited taste in food as she would only eat brown bread and drink tea!

Obviously something had to be done about that; it had sustained her after she had been abandoned but she now needed a more nutritious diet. Although we tried hard to tempt her with other foods she was just not interested.

Then, after a few days of settling her in, she and I went out into the garden and sat on the lawn. In one hand I held a slice of brown bread and in the other some cheese. I offered her a piece of the bread which, when she went to take it I withdrew, substituting the cheese instead which she at first refused. Eventually she realized that she had to eat the cheese before she could have the bread. It was a great relief when stage one, just getting her to eat something other than brown bread, was completed.

Gradually, over the weeks, larger portions of cheese were eaten and correspondingly smaller pieces of bread. Nipper never would eat meat, fish or poultry throughout the whole of her life with us.

Her meals consisted of Bonios, of which she was very fond, biscox, marrow bone biscuits and Frolic, which was at least a form of dried protein. But as time went on, so great was Nipper's love of digestive biscuits that visitors to our home used to bring her a packet of them!

On one of our annual visits to the vet for innoculations, I mentioned that I was worried that she refused to eat items of food which I thought were essential for canine well being. He told me that Nipper was a healthy little thing and that owners who insisted on buying expensive cuts of meat for their dogs caused far more problems to their pets' health - dogs' stomachs are unable to cope with such rich food.

Her diet became quite a talking point and she acquired fame as the vegetarian dog. A friend said to me after offering her meat and it was refused, "Whatever did they do to her? She must have been brutally treated."

A reminder of Nipper's early life was in her habit of peeping out from a hiding place, the side of a cupboard while her food was being prepared. She watched where her bowl was placed, then revealed herself, walked over to the bowl and ate. Slowly she acquired enough confidence to come and stand by me, overtly watching and taking an interest in the preparation of her meal. It was about this time that her coat changed. There was a noticeable improvement. The hard spikes yielded to a firm but softer fur.

## BIFFIN THE COMPOST DOG

The hero of our next tale has certainly come a long way from his days at The Blue Cross Home at Tiverton where, six years ago, he was left with his black mongrel friend George. The two dogs were homed separately and Biff, as he was then called, aged about four went to live at Lympstone Exmouth with Jenepher Allen who changed his name to Biffin. (Biffin is an old variety of Norfolk cooking apple)

During his happy years with Jenepher, Biffin has been by sea to the Scilly Isles, by train to Yorkshire, stayed at many B&B's up and down the country, learned to trot alongside Jenepher's bicycle, met HRH Prince Charles, and been photographed in "The Daily Telegraph".

Jenepher is an enthusiastic volunteer on the local composting team and Biffin always joins in the fun, sometimes not being able to resist the odd pilfered biscuit or pork pie from unwary fellow workers! Biffin also is very good at letting his mistress know if there are any rats to be sorted out.

In 2003 Lympstone campaigned vigorously against planned changes by DEFRA on schemes such as theirs, resulting in some press coverage. Biffin made sure he was in the centre of any pictures taken and behaved impeccably.

**Biffin**

## BEN

Mr J W Chapman of Shaldon writes to me about his faithful Old English Sheepdog Ben. Sadly Ben died just before his master saw my letter in Western Morning News requesting tales of rescued dogs. In writing about him I hope it may have helped Mr Chapman in his grief over losing his much loved pet.

Ben was rescued from a North Wales breeder and when I picked him up from the rescue centre near Honiton, at the Stockland Kennels, he could have been mistaken for a whippet, nothing more than a bag of bones plus sores and hardly any motivation for a two-year-old dog. He sat on my lap all the way home with his front paws on my shoulders licking my face so that when we arrived home I was covered in his saliva!

He had previously been called Ossy which we changed straight way to Ben and from that day on he became my shadow. We nursed him back to health with all the right food and nutrition until he became to look more like an Old English Sheepdog.

I think he had been very badly ill treated by his former owners because whenever I took my fishing rods out to clean them he would slink away, cringing low on his stomach in anticipation of the blows that were to follow. Anything resembling a stick had to be hidden away from him at that time.

He had his own bed but soon took a liking to my armchair so that he could look out of the window and bark at anyone he did not care for - like the postman or paper boy. I enjoy walking and every day we would walk for two miles round the lanes.

Sadly, Ben had a heart attack and died last week and he is now up in the big kennels in the sky.

**Ben**

I think he was aged about ten and he is greatly missed by all in the family.

## WALLY

Another Border Collie story from Iris Peakman of Exmouth.

Wally was rescued from the Blue Cross adoption centre at Tiverton when he was about twenty-five months old. This was in 1998 and when Iris took him home with her he was very timid and traumatized. Staff at the centre said he had been very badly treated and kicked round the head.

It took a lot of Iris's patience and devotion to win his confidence, even though they had jelled at first sight. He had to know that he would never be abused or abandoned again. He seemed to be very scared of men and would not go near one, not even friends or neighbours. If he saw anyone in the street who reminded him of his abusers his hackles would go up. This went on for several years.

After a few weeks Iris took him on a train journey, as her previous dog had loved a train ride. The train stopped at a local marine centre and about twenty commandos got on. Iris wondered how Wally would react. The men fed him titbits and Wally was fine - perhaps it was because they were in a large friendly group and from that moment he started to improve.

During the following year Wally chewed up everything in sight in spite of being given bones to gnaw. After he had chewed an electric cable the vet advised to put him into a cage whilst on his own. Wally loved it, he felt secure from the world in there - it was his and no one else's. He would disappear into it uninvited and Iris never used to worry about leaving him on his own if she went out.

He suffered a colitis problem for a time and also epilepsy, which has now very much improved.

Wally has a loving, gentle nature, is good with children, cats and other dogs and even tolerates Iris's two budgies.

He loves the telephone and the postman and races Iris to get there first. The sea has no appeal to him - he doesn't even paddle. He does love the garden and likes to sit next to his mistress while she is busy.

He also helps with fund-raising and wears his RSPCA coat with pride on street collection days, turning his head from side to side when spoken to.

He visits local residential homes and is a favourite with the inmates.

**Wally**

Like all dogs he has a built-in clock and knows when it is meal times. He has his own armchair opposite Iris and sleeps on her bed at night. It's certainly a life of luxury for Wally these days and doesn't he deserve it?

## KALEY

Cindy Fearns' little rescue dog Kaley was very lucky to have escaped serious injury when he fell from the flat above Cindy's office where she was working at the time.

At that time Kaley was living up in the flats with his lady owner. The owner's son had taken his mother out for a car ride and Kaley, left inside the flat, pushed the window open and jumped out!

Cindy saw what she thought was a door-mat go flying past the window. Fortunately Kaley hit the hedge, righted himself and landed on the grass. He started to walk up the road and Cindy and a colleague abandoned their work and ran after him. Cindy managed to touch his rear end, and although he was very frightened he did not attempt to bite her. Instead he turned round and followed them both back to the office, where he sat curled up at Cindy's feet for the rest of the afternoon.

When his owner returned home she was horrified at what had happened.

Later on Kaley pulled his owner over and she decided she would have to part with him, so back he went to kennels for the second time. His first owners had had a young baby and couldn't cope with him.

However it was third time lucky for Kaley. When Cindy returned from her holiday the Dog Warden contacted her and said she could have Kaley if she wanted him. Phone calls to the kennels were made and a few days later Cindy and her husband went to collect him and brought him home.

Cindy recalls "He looked so sad when we arrived for him, then he slowly climbed into the car and sat up as I started talking to him.

When we arrived home he followed us into our garden and stood looking up at the trees and the sky. That was two years ago, and he has been so good and has settled into our lives. It seems as if he has been with us forever".

**Kaley**

## BESSIE

Bessie is a Bassett Hound. She belongs to my friend Pam Fallowes, who sometimes spends her holidays in Sidmouth where she loves to walk in The Byes.

Bessie was an ex-brood bitch and was retired from breeding about five years ago. Pam believes her to be about ten. Poor Bessie had always lived a rather boring existence in an outside kennel block so, when she came to live with Pam, she found herself in the lap of luxury. She was not house-trained at this stage but with much patience Pam persevered and was eventually successful.

Bessie has a lovely placid, gentle nature and loves people and other dogs. She shares her home with a large black fluffy cat called Marley and the two animals tolerate each other. She is rather possessive of her bed if any one goes near it: she has never had a proper bed of her own before. She is now becoming rather lazy in her later years and so her increasing weight is a problem. She tends to be a rather greedy old lady! She had a back problem in July 2000 and had to stay at the vet's for eight days.

I recall Pam telling me a little story about Bessie when she had not had her for very long.

One day she was walking at a local beauty spot when two suspicious-looking men appeared, accompanied by several Lurcher dogs. Pam ignored them

**Bessie**

and walked on, thinking that Bessie was still ambling along behind her. However, after a while she turned round to look for her and realized with alarm that Bessie was nowhere to be seen. She spent an anxious few hours searching and calling for her and then decided to go back to where she'd left her car. No Bessie, so Pam sat in the car and waited. After a while the two men with their dogs came into view and there was naughty Bessie, trundling cheerfully behind them with her long thick tail waving gaily in the air. She looked very pleased with herself and must have had a lovely time hunting with those two lurchers!

Bessie leads a contented life with her routine of mostly eating and sleeping. She is well known and loved in the village where she lives and likes to greet her human and canine friends when she takes her daily walk.

## BARNEY

Barney, a beautiful Welsh Springer Spaniel, is another dog now living inside a house with a family, after always being kept in kennels.

Sam Shaw adopted Barney from the Blue Cross Centre, Tiverton, in August 1997. He was then aged two. He was an ex-gun dog and his owners were splitting up, so poor Barney was looking for another home.

Barney has, according to his proud owner Sam, turned out to be a fantastic companion dog. He loves to sleep on the bottom bunk of her younger son's bed and enthusiastically joins in camping trips, football and swimming. In fact,

**Barney**

Barney more or less runs the entire household, keeping everyone in order!

His favourite pastime is to watch the fish in the pond - Sam calls it Barneyvision.

He is simply a sensitive, loving character whom the family would be lost without.

Sam has recently adopted another dog, a young x collie retriever named Boots, and after a period of fun and games and mayhem they have now settled down together.

## MITZI

Barbara Glanfield lives in Cornwall but her little Yorkshire Terrier Mitzi came all the way from Bedfordshire to find a loving new home.

Barbara writes about Mitzi:

Mitzi has been part of our family now for eight and a half years. She came from a Yorkie rescue and rehoming centre in Bedford.

There were many little Yorkies of all shapes and sizes. Mitzi ran straight in, toy cracker in her mouth; all the other dogs were lovely, but she was special. She was blind in one eye but this did not seem to bother her.

She is now 14 years old, almost blind in both eyes and a little deaf, plus wonky knees. None of this stops her from running round the garden, barking with joy.

She is the sweetest little dog, always looking out for me and my husband if we are ever poorly or need comfort. She has a large basket of toys which she races to get to, after being let out and having had her breakfast, usually about 5.30 am. So we sit up in bed, bleary eyed, drinking our tea and playing with Mitzi and her Tigger Tiger.

We are convinced we are Mitzi's pets really!

### Comment from Jenny:

I have a small Yorkshire Terrier aged 15 called Gemma. Barbara's story strikes a chord.

For the last eighteen months we are woken up by Gemma, at any time from 4 am onwards. yapping persistently for her breakfast! This of course wakes up our other two dogs, Guy the Wire Fox Terrier and Hetty the Airedale, who also join in the dawn chorus. What we devoted pet owners put up with from our canine chums' whims and fancies!

**Mitzi**

## POPPY AND MOLLY

The Porters' first rescue dog, Poppy, was acquired from a local vet eleven years ago. She was seven months old and the young single mother who owned her could not cope with a lively pup living in a flat. She also had three children under school age and although Poppy had not been ill treated in any way it was obviously not an ideal environment for her to grow up in. Poppy is a lovely quiet ladylike dog and very passive in temperament.

Molly the other rescue dog had quite a different history behind her. She is now six years old, and when her picture appeared in the paper when she was only twelve weeks, Diane Porter and her husband fell in love with her and knew she was the dog for them. Poor Molly had been put in a black bin liner and left at the side of the A30.

It took several years, and lots of patience, to restore this little dog's confidence. The first year was horrendous, as she was so traumatised that she nipped her new owners' legs and chewed her way through a cane suite, two steering wheels and gear sticks, and many other things. The kennels who had taken her in thought she may have been picked up by her head and had been cruelly abused by the family who had first owned her. It took a while before she would allow her head to be touched and even now does not like her front under-arms touched. She loves to travel in the car but has to have her comfort blanket, which she sucks and chews constantly (a legacy of the bin bag incident, probably).

Molly and Poppy get on so well and give great joy and love to their devoted owners. Both are totally different in character - Poppy passive and obedient, Molly strong, boisterous and likes to be in charge. We have to remind her now and then that she is a dog, not a human!

**Molly and Poppy
with their owners Mr and Mrs Porter**

## SAM

The Tonkin family from Sidmouth has many fond memories of their late rescued Golden Labrador, Sam.

Pat Tonkin writes:

We rescued Sam from a lady living in Sidmouth called Mrs Shrimpton. Sam had at first been living in Exeter with a family who were breaking up: they couldn't manage three dogs so Sam had to go. Poor Sam was originally found tied up by wire outside the RSPCA Shelter on a hot August day; the family had taken him in and one of the young girls was very sad to see him go to yet another home.

**Sam with Mandy and the family cats**

We took Sam home. He was meant for my daughter - my husband had only gone to look, not thinking I would bring him home! Luckily he settled straight away and did not make any fuss about being in a strange place.

Sam was beautiful but a handful - he hated other dogs and had to be on the lead at all times. However, on Mondays I would walk with my girl friends and their four dogs, which he did not seem to mind. We would go out in the country and walk for about six miles. I would let Sam off and one minute he was there and then in the blink of an eye he would be off, chasing after wildlife! We would spend ages calling him before returning home without him.

Eventually someone would phone to say they had found him, fed him, and he was quite happy!

One day he disappeared and was found by a man in Newton Poppleford who was on his way to hospital in Exeter, so Sam went with him and I picked him up from there - he was a lovely man and I spent some time chatting to him.

We would often walk at East Hill Strips outside Sidmouth from where he disappeared three times. I had to go home because my friends had driven me and could wait no longer. However, Sam would arrive home via the local petrol filling station, where he would always stop off and then be driven home in the land rover.

Sam was a good house dog. We had three rescued cats as well and he tolerated them, but they had to eat their food up fast for if we turned our backs Sam would nudge them out of the way and finish off theirs as well. When he died the cats became fussy with their food, would leave it and come back later, demanding fresh.

Sam did not like the postman or the dustman and once we had a letter from the Postmaster General to say that we must keep him under control as he had leapt up at the postman. Once we had a new kitchen fitted and I had to go to work, so left the man fitting the units. When he went out to his van Sam would not let him back into the house - a neighbour phoned me and I had to come back home and let the poor man back in again.

He followed me everywhere when I was doing the housework. If I went out he would sit on the drive and wait for me to return. My daughter would creep up behind me and pretend to strangle me and Sam would growl to warn me. She would also play hide and seek with him around the house. Mandy was dedicated to him, and took him out every day even though he had to be on a lead and he was very strong for her to hold. She loved animals and would save up her pocket money and send it to the RSPCA unbeknown to us.

Sadly Sam caught Fox's Mange with complications and we were advised by the vet to put him to sleep. My husband and children clubbed together and had a portrait painted from his photograph and gave it to me for my birthday, so I still see him around. We will never forget him - he was a great and lovable character.

## DAN AND WILLS

Bill and Babs Le Gros used to live in Letchworth, Hertfordshire before they moved to Sidmouth several years ago. It was while they were living in Letchworth that they acquired Dan, their first rescue dog – left, while still a puppy, at the gate of the local Blue Cross Centre.

Dan was a small black and tan terrier cross breed and he lived happily with Bill and Babs for a number of years. Eventually the Le Gros's moved to Sidmouth.

Bill and Babs were the first of many friends I have made since buying a property in Sidmouth six years ago. I first met Babs on the train to Honiton as I travelled to Sidmouth looking for a house. The conversation soon turned to dogs and we quickly established a sympathetic rapport. Little Dan, who by then was quite elderly, was unwell at the time and Babs had cut short her visit to her son in order to come back to be with him.

**Dan**

**Wills**

Eventually Dan was put to sleep and Babs and Bill were anxious to obtain another rescued pet. They went to The Little Valley Rescue Centre and fell for the charms of Wills, a handsome Lurcher aged approximately one year. He had been rescued from a gipsy encampment and was in a poor state.

When Babs and Bill brought him home he was very reluctant to come inside the house, having only been used to an outdoor existence. He soon overcame his fears and now has settled into his lovely new home with his loving owners.

## HOLLY

Dorothy Ladlow of Tavistock wrote to me about Holly, her little Collie bitch.

I lost my Border Collie in January 2003 and was naturally devastated but determined to replace her as soon as possible.

Not far from where Dorothy lives there is a church on the top of Brentor Hill. The church has a car park and here on Christmas Eve 2002 a Collie bitch had been dumped in a basket. The poor dog had recently had puppies and it was only by chance that a horse rider out on his horse on Christmas morning found her shivering under the hedge. He contacted the police who rang the rescue centre and the owner of the centre came out and collected the dog, even interrupting his Christmas dinner!

**Holly**

The little waif was in a poor state and had not moved from her basket all day. The centre did their best for her, the local vet checked her over, and despite being underweight and having recently given birth she soon made a quick recovery. Dorothy heard about her and went to the rescue centre to see her and brought her home to see if she would settle down with her and her husband.

Dorothy and her husband took a long while feeding her correctly and grooming her coat to get her back to complete fitness and health.

They were rewarded for their effort and loving care by Holly, as she is now called, winning first prize in a local dog show.

Dorothy concludes: Holly is now part of the family. How any one could abandon a dog like this is beyond my comprehension, but she is all right now and she knows it!

## RUPERT

Seventeen years ago Jo Avati visited the RSPCA kennels in Birmingham, seeking a replacement pet for her little dog who had just died. There were plenty to choose from but suddenly Jo saw a shivering little wreck in a corner of a cage.

**Rupert**

Another lady was interested in him but passed on to look at the other dogs. He was such an ugly little scrap. There were numbers and letters on his cage and Jo asked the kennel maid what they meant. "Vet to come at 11.40 am to put him to sleep" the girl replied. Jo's mind was at once made up; she paid the fee of £11, and returned with her daughter the following day to collect him. Jo's daughter looked horrified as he was brought out to meet them. He had the high stepping gait of a whippet and the hindquarters of a bull terrier, which did nothing for his looks!

Jo took him home and introduced him to her two other bitches and called in the vet. Rupert, as Jo christened him, had six toes on his front feet and untreated dew claws. The vet estimated him to be about eighteen months old and recommended he should have a bath!

Rupert became very close to Jo during the seventeen happy years they spent together.

He had an extremely eventful life – once, when Jo's back was turned, fathering fourteen pups in one go! However, all ended happily and Jo is left now with many happy memories of her little waif from the RSPCA kennels at Birmingham.

## TOMMY

Tommy was a well-known popular canine inhabitant of Sidmouth. Everyone knew him in the town, where one day he certainly left his mark!

He belonged to Phillip Margaret, a hair stylist in Temple Street. Phillip rescued him from an animal shelter near Exeter when he was about three years old. He was a medium-sized brown x breed, with a perky expression.

Although Tommy liked to sit in Phillip's salon, where he was popular with the clients, he was also an expert escape artist and would disappear to the town and sea front at the least opportunity. One of Philip's clients, an animal lover who lived nearby, would often have unofficial visits from

**Tommy**

Tommy - once he entered her house through the cat flap!

One day there was a plaque-laying ceremony on Sidmouth seafront. Tommy was out on his travels that day and with typical curiosity decided to trot along the front to see what was going on. Just at the critical moment, as the plaque was put in place and the local important dignitaries stood around watching and applauding, Tommy appeared, casually raised his hind leg and christened the plaque with due ceremony, before disappearing from the scene in search of more mischief!

He lived to the ripe old age of fifteen, his later years confined to the salon where he used to sit and snooze, no doubt dreaming of his former escapades.

## MEG

Another lucky rescued brood bitch now lives with Stewart Webb of Colaton Raleigh.

Stewart writes: "I had been looking for a rescued Springer Spaniel for about ten months when I first heard about Meg. A customer at the filling station where I am manager had a friend working at the Bristol RSPCA. He was in regular

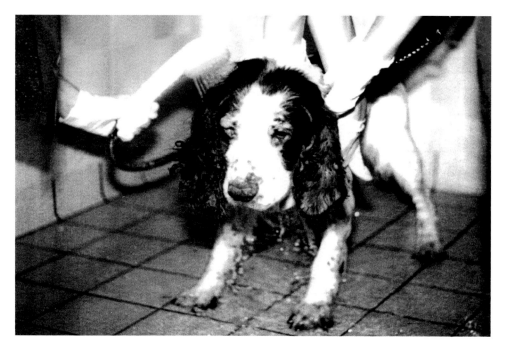

**Bath time for Meg**

contact with her and she had said that a Springer Spaniel had been brought in by the local police. She had been found wandering the streets and was in a terrible state. To quote the RSPCA 'She wouldn't win a beauty contest!'

She had ear, eye, skin and womb infections and also mange. It was only her lovely nature that saved her from being put to sleep.

After many phone calls we made the trip to Bristol. At first she did not want to know me, but after some nice walks and tasty treats we started to bond. After six weeks of recuperation, and after several visits, I was allowed to take her home and now, six and a half years later, we are still together.

Her previous history is unknown. The vets at Bristol believe she was an ex-puppy farm breeding bitch who could not have any more litters and so was kicked out. She had a recent scar on her stomach which 'may have been the result of a caesarian operation'.

Meg may not have won a beauty contest but we all think she is beautiful enough to be our choice of cover girl for "Wag Tales".

**Meg as she is today**

## NELL

Ken and Pauline Line of Woodbury Salterton now own Nell, a failed sheepdog, abandoned by a farmer to a rescue centre because she was frightened of the sheep!

Nell had had quite a traumatic life until she finally found love, peace and calm with Ken and Pauline.

After she left the farm the rescue centre fostered her out to a young lady who, after keeping her for one week, returned her to the farmer instead of back to the centre. It was assumed he kept her in a barn with other dogs, which resulted in Nell having a litter of eight puppies after her first season. The centre fortunately heard about her plight and recovered her once more, and it was there she actually gave birth to the litter.

When Ken and Pauline first went to see Nell all of the pups had been re-homed at eight weeks, bar one. Nell was very thin, with bare patches, but as she walked up to her new owners her whole body wagged and wriggled and they knew she was the dog for them.

**Nell**

She settled in with the other dog in the family, Bliss, and they eat and sleep together, but she is still wary of Ted the cat. After five months in her lovely new home all Nell wants to do is play, after having had no proper puppyhood until now.

Pauline is at present taking her to training classes and she is starting to socialize well with other dogs.

Ken concludes: "Nell's coat has now grown, she is a lovely fluffy girl and she gives us lots of love and affection".

## CHARLIE

Margaret Ryalls from Newton Poppleford visited The RSPCA Little Valley Shelter looking for a companion dog for her Labrador x Collie, Megan.

She was first shown a dog similar to Megan but he was not at all friendly to her. So then Margaret saw 1-year-old Charlie, a Springer Spaniel x collie, left at the centre by a young mother unable to cope with a dog.

Charlie had obviously decided Margaret and her husband were the right owners for her and tried to wriggle under the cage door to get to them. It was love at first sight, and Megan and Charlie bonded well together.

Charlie had to be spayed before going to her new home and when she first arrived she was very nervous. She wouldn't leave Margaret's side and was very difficult to control on a lead. However she responded well to praise and was very eager to please. Being a spaniel she is a bit of a greedy girl and can be a bit naughty when food is around!

Charlie and Margaret go to obedience, agility and heelwork to music classes, which both of them enjoy. Her favourite walks are by the river.

Margaret writes "Charlie is a joy to have around, her temperament is lovely and calm. Sadly we lost Megan earlier this year and Charlie missed her for a while, they were great friends. However she brings great comfort, companionship and delight to my husband, who is disabled - especially when I am not there."

**Charlie**

# The following four contributions are from members of the Sidmouth Poetry Readers

## CHOPPER AND SMOKEY

Mike Baker, a member of Sidmouth Poetry Readers, and his wife, Thelma, had a sad start to 2005 when their dog Chopper died aged thirteen. Chopper was of mixed parentage, his mother an Alsatian x Border Collie and his father a Labrador x Pitbull Terrier. Chopper was one of a litter of unwanted puppies rescued from travellers in Maidstone, Kent.

Poor Chopper lost an eye in 2000 and had an operation for testicular cancer in 2004. He had to be put to sleep eventually due to cancer of the spleen, with kidney problems.

However despite his unfortunate health problems of later years, Chopper had a very happy life with his master and mistress. According to Mike he was an extremely laid back dog who got on well with the family cat, Mollie.

Smokey the lurcher, the Bakers' new rescue bitch, is however very different in nature and is proving to be quite a challenge!

Smokey was seen on SW TV early in 2005. She was at The Little Valley Animal Shelter. Very much like Chopper in appearance - only rough coated with dark patches, hence her name - she had some Alsatian in her, and her tail was bushy and curled over her back.

She was about four years old and had been dumped by her first owner on a friend, hoping he or she would care for her. But the friend did not want her and so took her to the Animal Shelter.

Mike and Thelma inspected Smokey carefully; she was frantically looking at everyone passing by. There was a small dog in her pen with whom she was playing.

The supervisor at the shelter said that she was a nervous dog but OK with other dogs. This however was not quite an accurate description of Smokey.

Mike writes:

Smokey is terrified of loud bangs - presenting quite a problem living near the

**Chopper with family and friend**

Marine Rifle Range. It is therefore not possible to walk her nearby when there is target practice.

She lives with the cat but chases after her when Mollie retreats - who now sleeps upstairs and stays out all night. Mollie tried to be friendly to her by brushing against her legs as she used to with Chopper. However this only happened once and now the dog and cat only eat together, nose to nose: the food obviously distracting Smokey's attention. Afterwards they have to be separated again.

Her nervousness manifests itself if she suddenly sees anyone dressed or behaving oddly, and she rushes at the person concerned, barking furiously. If someone approaching on a walk puts their dog on the lead ahead of her she will pretend to attack it, or if any sudden movement occurs she will jump or react. She will however wait for eight minutes while being tied up before starting to bark!

Retraining Smokey has proved tricky. She now does not pull on the lead, and will wait

**Smokey**

and come when called, but sudden sallies on other dogs - especially those which respond with aggression - is still a problem.

Smokey is a very affectionate playful dog, even her cat chasing is just for fun and she is not in any way aggressive. She runs fast and loves to "skylark."

Mike concludes that on the whole Smokey is a good find and although not the same as Chopper, who was an exceptional pet companion, certainly keeps her new owners on their toes. Good for physical health perhaps, not so much for mental!

## DANNY

Elizabeth Strickland, another member of the Sidmouth Poetry Readers, has owned many rescued dogs and cats. Her present pets are two cats named Planet and Comet, and Danny, a Golden Labrador Cross

Danny came from the Blue Cross and was about four years old when Elizabeth adopted him eight years ago.

Elizabeth writes:

Danny must be about twelve now, he is getting a bit grey but can still run like a racing greyhound.

He was well trained in some ways when I got him, though not always obedient, very good when tied, and in the car. I don't use the dog guard which I had for previous dogs, and he never jumps across from the boot. Danny loves visitors and can be rather over enthusiastic in greeting people who come to the house.

Recently Comet the cat has taken to sleeping with Danny in his chair. If she is in the chair first he won't get in, but I turn her out, and he gets in and curls round. Then she gets in behind him and lies along his back. They sometimes sleep like that all night.

The photograph on the next page is of Comet on the fence, with **Danny**.

Elizabeth also offers this advice and encouragement to owners introducing a new dog to resident cats. It was published in The Cats Protection League Newsletter.

In July 1995 I adopted two kittens. I named them Planet and Comet. When they came to me I had a Labrador x Collie who was good and gentle with them. Just as they were getting brave enough to play with his tail, he was taken ill and died. I did not replace him for several months, so the kittens grew up in a dogless home.

On my second visit to the Blue Cross at Bickleigh I found Danny, a Labrador x. He looks like a golden thick-set greyhound, and his CV said 'good with cats', so I took him.

He chased those cats at every opportunity! Luckily I had a wooden fence up which they could escape. However, right from the first there was a truce at night; we all sleep in one room, Danny in a chair and the cats on my bed, and he's never interfered with them.

Of course I tried to stop Danny chasing the cats, and always scolded him when he did. If I took him for a free run in the fields opposite, he would elude me and chase the cats up the drive. But they soon learned how to outwit him.

My drive runs parallel to next door's, with only a stranded wire fence in between. The cats learned that if they ran up next door's drive, Danny would bash his face on the wire - once he nearly lost an eyebrow!

If they ran in different directions, he lost time in deciding which one to chase, and recently they have learned not to run at all, but just sit still while Danny goes hurtling past! So they obviously know that he means them no ill. Comet will even rub herself against Danny's front legs.

The helpful booklet that the Blue Cross gave me said "Your cat will get to know your dog in its own way, this can sometimes take months". It did, but now we are one happy family.

**Comet, on the fence, with Danny**

# PRINCE

Dr Stewart Gordon and his wife Jean are great animal lovers and have owned a variety of dogs all their married life. At the moment they share their Sidmouth home with Topsy, their West Highland Terrier, and Trudie, the Cairn terrier belonging to their daughter Catherine. Sometimes Stewart and Jean look after Murphy, a friend's Rhodesian Ridgeback. However, the family treasure fond memories of Prince, a little rescued mongrel from some years back. Stewart who is a member of the Sidmouth Poetry Readers has written two delightful poems in memory of faithful Prince.

### MY DOG PRINCE

*I found my dog Prince at the Rescue Home*
*A long time since. His former name was Jeff,*
*But this was changed to Prince.*
*Our friends had suggested Billy, Billy do*
*They said it had a touch of class.*
*But at Dog Obedience, he only gained a pass.*
*Of course he would obey any command*
*Like "Come" "Heel" "Sit Down" and "Stand".*
*When you said "Go" he'd really go*
*And weave through sticks like Billy O*
*Run up ramps, fly through the air*
*Surmounting every barrier, it really was spectacular*
*He'd leap through hoops, dash through the tunnel*
*He was really quite phenomenal and could have won the*
*                                    prized gold medal*
*And received it stood smartly at attention.*
*But so far I've failed to mention*
*The one command Prince would not obey*
*Where the owner has to go away and leave his dog*
*For up to about twenty minutes say,*
*The one they call EXTENDED stay*
*Prince's response to this was "No way No way"*
*His limit was about a minute.*
*I tried to get him to stay put, like any other kind of mutt*
*But after sustained exposition and much talking*
*His maintained position was "You must be joking".*
*He would insist on finding me which he could do unerringly*
*Without command. You didn't even have to tell him "FIND"*
*He knew exactly what he had in mind.*
*He was so good and strong and fast*

*And would defend me to the last.*
*His proper name was Prince*
*We haven't been to Dog Obedience since*
*Prince really had that touch of class*
*Although he only ever gained a pass*
*Now you may think that all of this is quite unfair –*
*but my dog Prince just didn't care*
*I'd found him and he'd found me*
*And that's the way it had to be.*


## IN GREEN PASTURES

*Lord, I keep watch!*
*If I am not there who will guard their house*
*Watch over their sheep? Be faithful?*
*No One but You and I know what faithfulness is.*

Anon from  *"The Prayer of the Dog"*


## BELOVED PRINCE - by Stewart Gordon

*Beloved Prince*
*Beloved by me,*
*It would be no life for me*
*Unless I thought*
*That I should see*
*You once again*
*Running free for evermore*
*Through grassy fields*
*Or by the shore*
*And things would be*
*For you and me*
*Just as before*
*Beloved Prince*
*Beloved by me*
*Your spirit fills my memory*

**Prince**

## GEORGE

Margot Collingbourn-Beevers is also a member of the Sidmouth Poetry Readers, and a former Chair. Here is her poem dedicated to her late, dearly-loved Black Labrador, George, who died on 23 March 2003. George was born and bred in a stable, but he soon adapted to a home environment. He always loved wide, open spaces where he could run madly at will, but he was never happy out of sight of his owners.

### *REQUIEM FOR GEORGE - 1990-2003*

*A world-emptiness on waking. No George now,*
*today or ever. No greeting run on our return.*
*No splashing leap in sea or summer stream.*
*So much our days you were, and in our sleeping.*
*You were so always with us, in the field, by the fire,*
*that young dog leaping in the Cotswold snow,*
*circling in happy wonder on a beach in Wales;*
*delighting in the Devon seas and moors, the routine days.*
*And so much more you gave: such love and loving.*
*Always you were that pure black shining thread that ran*
*for us through each day's tasking. Through our tears*
*we will bless you in our mind's eye, we will treasure*
*all the wondrous days we loved you, loved the kindness*
*in your giving, the softening curve of your sleeping body.*
*Always we will recall, with simple, grateful memories,*
*how joyfully you shared with us your many years.*

Written at Candlemas Cottage, Sidford, Devon, the morning after George died.

© Margot Collingbourn-Beevers.

**George with Margot on the Gower Peninsula, South Wales**

# PAWS PATTER

*If you pick up a starving dog and make him prosperous*
*He will not bite you*
*This is the principal difference between dog and man.*

*Mark Twain*

During the eighties and nineties I helped a small animal rescue charity run by an elderly couple living in the Luton area. I often helped with fund-raising activities and also in helping to find homes for the endless stream of abandoned dogs, cats and other small pets.

Many of the dogs I looked after myself in my own boarding kennels; two of them, Oscar and Alice, spent the rest of their lives with me. There are far too many to mention in this book but here are just five of the many waifs and strays for whom I was responsible for finding homes.

## BEN

Little Ben had never heard a kind word or known love during the first three years of his life.

I collected him from an estate in Luton notorious for violence and crime. The family who were getting rid of him said he was vicious and uncontrollable. I brought him back to my home, where I settled him into the kennels. He proved to be a typical Jack Russell, noisy, full of fighting spirit and defiant. But the reason for his anti-social behaviour was, as in most cases, fear. He had obviously been cruelly abused in his former home. I recall how he half dragged me down the path away from the slamming front door when I picked him up.

I think we tried several lines of action. I took him to the vet first, to have him neutered. I'd hoped to home him with another dog and the operation would probably in time, help to calm him down.

Then on impulse I rang the local newspaper and spoke to Eric, the friendly journalist who often ran articles on our charity, which had frequently resulted in our homing a dog or cat. I knew Eric had a small brown and white Jack Russell called Charlie and he wrote a little column about Charlie and his doings every week. He called it Tail Piece.

I told Eric about Ben and he was very interested. "Shall have to ask the wife first", he said cheerfully. "Would she mind another dog" I queried anxiously. "Leave it to me" Eric replied, "Maureen grew up on a farm and owned five Jack

Russells at one time!"

Here was hope indeed. I took Ben round to Eric's house the next day, praying for a happy outcome. It was ideal. Eric and Maureen were a happy-go-lucky couple with three lovely teenage children. They all made Ben welcome and the poor little chap responded with enthusiasm, the first happy environment he'd known.

Then came the crunch - Ben was introduced to Charlie. At first there was a bit of cautious sniffing and wary murmurings from each side. Then, a truly magical moment when, to our joy, both stumpy tails started to wag furiously, leads were released and the two dogs became firm friends. As time went on Ben, according to Eric, followed the older, placid-natured Charlie everywhere, gaining in self-confidence as the months passed. Eric often mentioned Ben's early days in his Tail Piece, usually an anecdote about naughty Ben's latest antic; it was often to do with food.

I think a padlock had to be fixed on the kitchen fridge until Charlie had taught Ben better manners.

# Best paws forward for animal welfare

IF YOU take your dog for a walk on Sunday afternoon, why not join Charlie the Jack Russell and me in the sponsored dog walk round Wardown?

Starting at 2 pm we will be striding round and round Wardown Lake to raise cash for PAWS, the Phone Animal Welfare Society, which will be used to help stray and homeless dogs, and to build an animal sanctuary in the town. I am told that every dog taking part will receive a reward, with prizes offered for the dog doing the most circuits of the lake, the youngest and oldest dogs taking part, etc.

Every dog on the march will also receive a Luton News certificate recording their efforts.

Charlie is looking forward to leading the parade, and to rubbing shoulders with one of the top dogs in the country.

Sharing the limelight with our Jack Russell will be a Crufts champion from Dunstable, 'Obedience Champion Woughstock Wisdom' who is more commonly known as Jasper. Leading the seven-year-old border collie will be his proud owner, Beverley Hughes, of Leighton Court, Dunstable. Charlie, and our recent

Charlie and Ben – held by Eric – give an encore to PAWS dogs Daisy May and Oscar.

acquisition, big Ben who will also be aiding the cause, are both dogs that were rescued from being put down.

**Ben, Charlie and Oscar stepping out for PAWS**

## CANNON

Cannon was part Irish Terrier and he was taken into Dunstable Police Station after being found on the M1 in Bedfordshire after being thrown from a lorry. Mind you Cannon was a handful. He wasn't much more than a puppy at the time of this unfortunate incident.

However he settled quite happily and quietly into my kennels and I didn't think we would have too much trouble in finding him a home.

Time passed and still Cannon remained with me. He had the necessary op which calmed him down a little but it still did not solve his main fault of fighting other dogs. He would definitely have to be homed on his own.

One day when I was exercising him in our village I met my friend Nikki's two younger teenage daughters, Verity and Natasha. As bad luck had it they had had to have their border collie, Shannon, put to sleep recently for biting their father David twice. They were full of enthusiasm for Cannon, who rolled on his back and pedalled all four paws in the air, looking from one to the other, selling himself shamelessly.

"We'll go and ask Mum!" Off they flew, whooping and shrieking with excitement to tackle their unsuspecting parents, and I went home and once again prayed for luck in homing yet another difficult waif.

So the two girls talked their easy-going parents round and Cannon went to his new home, just round the corner.

Several nights later there was a ring on the front door bell; it was winter time and pitch black. Nikki, her eldest daughter Tracey, and Natasha stood on the doorstep, all three in floods of tears. Cannon had jumped the fence and disappeared into the night.

I put on my coat and joined Nikki in her car for the search. There was no sign of him anywhere. David, Nikki's husband, and Verity were in David's car cruising in another area.

It got very late, we were all exhausted and in tears. We agreed to go home in the hope that Cannon would eventually return home. I sat up late unable to go to bed to sleep, when all at once I heard a feeble scratch at the front door. I flew to open it and there stood Cannon, swaying on his feet and looking dazed and shaken. He'd been hit by a car but with typical terrier resilience and bloody-mindedness had eventually found his way home to me. Delighted, I rang Nikki and took him straight back, where he received a joyous welcome. The vet examined him the next day and pronounced him unhurt, just a little shaken.

David always said he was a survivor, and he was to be proved right a number of times in the fifteen happy years he lived with them.

David and Nikki moved from the village about five years ago and went to live on their ocean-going sailing boat. Cannon had his own passport and of course accompanied them, visiting many countries.

**Jenny with Cannon**

He'd certainly journeyed a long way from that MI in Bedfordshire!

## BILLY

I used to look after Billy in my boarding kennels when his owners went off on holidays.

I did not like Billy's owners. They made it clear from the start that they had only taken him on because their daughter, to whom he had belonged, had married and moved away leaving Billy, a miniature Yorkshire Terrier, for them to look after. He was a tiny scrap of a thing. I should think he barely weighed a couple of pounds.

Then for several years I did not see Billy. I concluded he must have died. I used to think about him often. One day the man who owned him rang up and booked him in for a ten days' stay while they went on holiday. "We've not been away for years" he said, as he left him with me. I was appalled at Billy's condition: he must by now have been about 14. He was thin and emaciated, had hardly any coat, and his teeth were rotting in his mouth.

He could probably not have managed to have eaten if he'd tried. I decided to employ cunning female strategy.

During the next ten days I managed to get him to eat, mostly scrambled eggs and soft brown bread and marmite sandwiches. He started to look better and a little more animated, less apathetic.

"That dog is not going back to that horrible couple!" I declared fiercely to Anthony my brother. "Whatever you say!" he agreed whole heartedly. He had to!

When the man arrived I met him at the front door and put on my most charming manner and smile. "Oh, Mr A you've come to collect Billy. Oh dear, I shall miss him - of all the dogs that come here he is my most favourite of all!". I gushed away for several moments before throwing in the trump card. "Please could I keep him here for myself, obviously I won't charge you for his holiday board."

The man thought for a few seconds then - "I'll have to phone the wife first" he said. "Oh please do, there's the phone!" and I almost frog-marched the poor man into the hall to make the call. I could not but help hear his shrewish spouse on the other end of the line and I almost certainly heard her say "good riddance!" or words to that effect.

So this dear inoffensive little old dog stayed with us for the next few months. The vet took all his teeth out after he was strong enough to take the op. With proper feeding he put on weight and his coat improved.

But we had a problem. Tom, our current Wire Fox Terrier at that time, was jealous and so Billy couldn't come into the house with him. He lived quite happily with our resident cats in the outside office for a time and then, quite unexpectedly, a wonderful opportunity occurred for him.

A very nice lady was collecting her two cats from the cattery one day and noticed him in the office. She said she had two just like him. I told her the story and there and then she offered to take him home with her.

It was a wrench but I tried to think of what was best for Billy. I think I would have been selfish to have kept him under the present circumstances.

So off he went with her and a few weeks later I visited him in his new home, which was a lovely old cottage on the Luton Hoo Estate.

He was in seventh heaven. There was Billy, with his two new Yorkie friends and the two cats. I believe he lived on there with that kind lady for another two years. Happy twilight years for a well-deserving little dog. (Billy is a pseudonym).

## LUKE

Luke was bought to me one day via Win, the owner of PAWS. He was a thoroughbred Saluki who had been abandoned by gypsies in the area. A beautiful gentle dog, he had a faraway, almost mystical, expression in his almond-shaped eyes.

He was in a very poor condition and I don't think he had ever been inside a house, so was not house trained. I estimated his age to be eighteen months. I had never had experience of the breed before and wondered whether they were anything like their cousins, the Afghan Hounds. I had boarded one once in my kennels, a rescued bitch owned by a district nurse. The dog's name was Sasha and she used to behave in an eccentric, erratic manner when on the lead. Without warning she would lie down in the gutter with her four paws in the air, it was almost impossible to get her to move until she was ready!

However Luke was totally different in nature, docile and eager to please and so grateful for being looked after. I could see that he would make a lovely pet for the right owner. He was intelligent and sensitive, needing the patience and dedication of someone who really loved and understood dogs.

**Luke with Jenny**

My cousin Michael called one day and immediately fell for Luke's aristocratic charm. Michael had lived on a farm all his boyhood and had always had a natural affinity with dogs. He asked if he could take Luke home for a trial period, as there were three cats in the household and his wife was not really used to dogs.

I agreed to this with mixed feelings. I did not know Michael's wife very well, I knew that she was at home all day and would have to bear the brunt of coping with any mishaps or accidents that might occur with Luke still not being house trained.

In less than a week Michael phoned to say that Luke was chasing the cats, being dirty in the house and generally causing uproar. So back he came to me and poor Michael bade him an emotional farewell at my front door.

I contacted Saluki Rescue as I could see that they were the best experienced in homing this particular dog. It would have been too traumatic for him to be returned to me again. A very sensible, capable lady arrived on my doorstep a few days after Michael had returned him to me and assured me that there would be no difficulty in placing him in a home with someone who had owned a Saluki before. She was right; a few weeks later he went to live with a family in Eastbourne and his worries were over.

## TRIXIE

Another rescue that came my way was Trixie, a dear black and tan terrier cross breed whose owner had had to part with her due to moving into a flat.

The little dog was about seven. She was a very sweet-natured dog and a lovely companion to have around. Re-homing her was easy and it wasn't long before she was happily settled in with her new owners, a retired couple Mr and Mrs M, who lived on the outskirts of Luton.

I often used to visit Trixie in her new home and was always given a warm welcome, both from her and her new owners.

Every year I used to look after her in my kennels while Mr and Mrs M went on their annual holidays, always to the same seaside resort and the same guest house. They were a dear couple, very conventional and well organized. When I used to collect Trixie she would be standing obediently at the door with her tartan dog bed, towel and her two plastic dishes to be packed into the car. The budgie would be waiting in his cage to be taken round to the next door neighbour.

There would then follow the same ritual which occurred year after year and never failed to amuse and intrigue me.

Mr M, never Mrs M, would take off Trixie's collar and replace it with another identical collar but with a lead attached. "That's her house collar, Mr M explained seriously as he put it away in a drawer. "she has one she wears around the house and the other that she goes out in." I've never come across this before, a special little indulgence for a much loved pet.

**Trixie**

Trixie lived to a good age and then passed away and Mr and Mrs M acquired Buster, a Lakeland Terrier.

By this time I was no longer boarding dogs so I never had him to look after. But every Christmas I receive a card and I am always reminded of dear Trixie, the dog with an inside and outside collar, and her owners Mr and Mrs M.

# SCRAPS

*Montmorency came and sat on things just as they were wanted*
*To be packed. He put his leg in the jam and he worried the tea spoons*
*And he pretended the lemons were rats, and got into the hamper and killed*
*three of them.*

Jerome K Jerome from "Three Men in a Boat"

> *Guy our Wire Fox Terrier,*
> *Four straight legs like a pendulum swing*
> *Retired people would point a finger and say*
> *"When I was young it was the thing*
> *To own one of those little chaps:*
> *They were popular in our day,*
> *But oh we had so many mishaps*
> *When they'd escape and run away.*
> *Dad would have his wallet handy*
> *To compensate for a slaughtered hen*
> *Or stand ready with the brandy*
> *When Gyp had chased Mrs. Brown's cat again.*
> *Then they were very popular*
> *Well, everything goes in trends,*
> *Now Westies, Yorkies and Cavaliers*
> *Head the list of man's small best friends".*

## ASTA

We have owned three wire haired Fox Terriers over the last thirty years. The first we named Asta, after the famous film star Terrier from the American detective series "The Thin Man". Asta, with his quirky and endearing ways, frequently stole the limelight from his human co-stars William Powell and Myrna Loy. The films were made during the thirties and forties when wire haired Terriers were at the height of their popularity.

One wet autumn afternoon as I was driving along the A6 into Luton I noticed a small scruffy white dog wandering along the middle of the road, looking vaguely up at the passing cars. I stopped my mini van, got out and spoke to the little dog, which turned out to be a wire fox Terrier. He was filthy dirty and in need of a hair cut! His colour was predominately white, except for one round black spot on his neck and another on his back near his tail. I opened the car door and without any persuading he leapt in, curled up, and went to sleep exhausted.

When I arrived home I telephoned the police with a description of the little dog, confident that there must be some very anxious owners somewhere who would be very relieved to have good news of their missing pet. The policeman checked the 'lost and found' list and said that a lady had reported a wire terrier missing that day from the Hitchin area and the description fitted my little waif exactly. I quickly phoned the number that the policeman gave to me and a man answered saying the dog had returned home that day. He then slammed down the receiver, abruptly ending the conversation. I could only conclude that the wife had reported the dog was missing and her husband didn't want him back - had probably done the dumping job himself. There could not have been two dogs of identical description missing on the same day within a ten-mile radius.

After discussing it with my parents we decided to stay quiet and keep him, so that was how Asta entered our life and became a faithful and loyal companion for the next eleven years.

"How could anyone want to be rid of such a lovely-natured handsome dog?" This was the question which we were frequently asked. The answer to the mystery soon became obvious; although a perfect gentleman with people, children included, and female dogs, he hated all male dogs and would start a fight on the smallest pretext, and follow it through to the end! We wondered how many vet bills had been presented to Asta's former owners by outraged injured parties.

I remember one afternoon in Ampthill Park, when we were blackberrying and had Asta safely on a lead. We were just making our way back to the car when we saw a retired couple with two beautiful Golden Retrievers coming towards us. The two retrievers were off the lead and on our approach sank to the ground on instant command from their well-spoken owners, and waved their long feathered tails in an affable greeting. The gentleman owner

**Asta**

raised his trilby to me and to my mother and murmured a polite good afternoon. Asta, on sighting the two dogs, let out a blood-curdling snarl and bared his snapping teeth in their direction. Mumbling an embarrassed apology to the couple I dragged the little fiend past as quickly as possible. I dread to think what would have happened if he'd been off the lead, as he often was. It was the one flaw in his make-up. In all other respects he was the best-natured and placid of the three wires we have owned. He loved the car and would travel happily anywhere with us on holiday, staying at hotels in the Lake District, Eastbourne, and Devon.

Many of the older generation would stop and chat to us on our walks and reminisce about terriers they themselves had owned in the past. The opening conversation usually began: "Oh, we had one of those when we were children at home back in the thirties, always in trouble escaping from the garden, fighting other dogs and chasing cats and killing hens. You would never let him off the lead or he'd be gone for days. Highly strung little chap. He was terrified of thunderstorms but a grand little character, good ratter too!" Asta would stand looking as if butter wouldn't melt in his mouth as he listened to his breed's praises being sung.

The interesting thing we noticed about the people we met was that they never mentioned having owned more than the one wire Terrier in their time. Once bitten perhaps!

## BOSUN

He would never have won first prize for the most handsome dog, not even in the mutt class!

His head was white and tan, terrier shaped, with a fox's brush-type tail. He had the overall look of the old-fashioned welsh collie but he was smaller in size, more like a corgi. His stumpy fore legs bowed outwards but it was his eyes which were most noticeable.

His right eye was a wall eye, ie blue in colour, which suggested Welsh collie ancestry. But the left eye was an angry, inflamed red, bulging from the socket the size of a ping-pong ball. It was an advanced neglected glaucoma.

Bosun was the fourth dog I had owned, and the second of my four rescued dogs. I found him trundling along the A6 towards Luton - in almost the same spot as I had found Asta, my wire Fox Terrier waif, several years before.

The eye needed immediate attention, so the next day I took him to my vet where he was examined by a young Scottish lady vet who had recently joined the practice. She judged him to be about thirteen and said the eye was causing him great pain and discomfort and would need to be removed. "Poor wee thing " she observed sympathetically "he won't stand much chance of getting a home down at the dog pound, not with his age and that awful eye, no wonder the owners turned him out!"

He had the eye removed the next day and it healed beautifully during the following weeks and all that could be seen afterwards was a small dimple in his white face. It added to the overall quirkiness of his appearance: he was certainly unique - there couldn't be another like him. Of course there was no question of his going to the dog pound, he was here to stay!

During the next few months his true character began to shine through. He was a plucky little fellow and would tackle any dog larger than himself if he took a dislike to it.

A vicar who lived nearby owned a small Jack Russell named Tigger, who roamed the district daily on various shady expeditions. He was known everywhere and was often accompanied on his adventures by the local doctor's Golden Retriever, Beth, and three other local dogs, Polly a Dalmatian, Pepsie a Boxer cross Labrador belonging to a solicitor, and Tess a black Labrador, also owned by a doctor. All of them young, flighty bitches and more than eager to follow Tigger into whatever trouble he could snout out! He was in fact rather like William in the Just William books by Richmal Crompton. Tess, Polly, Pepsie and Beth formed the rest of the outlaw gang!

The dogs would often vanish for the whole day causing their owners great anxiety. Once I remember Mrs B, Polly's owner, telling me she had stood up in her bedroom for nearly one whole day looking through binoculars for them to return. When they eventually turned up she noticed with amusement that the intrepid Tigger was lagging at the back with the female foursome out in front! Obviously the day's adventures had worn him out but he was still determined not to abandon his devoted entourage. "The trouble is" Mrs B's husband gloomily observed to me one day, "We don't know where they go, or what they get up to!" What indeed!

Bosun encountered Tigger one day in a nearby field; there was instant mutual hatred and all hell broke loose. The vicar's teenage son and daughter and I had to separate them, and it was not at all easy. Bosun had Tigger's scruff in a tight grip and the air was filled with shrieks, blood-curdling growls and colourful language, mostly from me because I knew Bosun had been the instigator. We parted them after what seemed like an eternity and, apologizing profusely to

John and Sarah who were very decent about the whole incident, dragged an unrepentant Bosun off home. We none of us escaped unscathed that day!

Several weeks later they met up again in the churchyard. Poor Tigger was trying to make a dignified exit with Bosun trotting briskly behind him with a purposeful expression on his grizzled white face. Tigger, with a look of nonchalant disregard, disappeared into the safety of his back garden and a very disappointed Bosun was led firmly home.

I only owned him for about two and a half years but he occupied a very special place in my heart. He began to develop fits as he grew older which became more and more frequent and severe. It was kindest to put him to sleep but right to the end the gallant little chap put up a brave fight. In the short while he spent with me he repaid me with great loyalty. Who were the heartless folk who had abandoned him? I shall never know.

**Asta and Bosun**

# HOLIDAY SNAPS

## BIMBO AND NIKKI

One of my favourite dogs, who used to stay at my boarding kennels back in the seventies, was a wire haired Terrier called Bimbo, who belonged to George and Madge Bott of Luton.

I remember when their first Fox Terrier, also named Bimbo, had to be put to sleep at the age of fourteen and the Botts were naturally very upset. He was always referred to as Bimbo Bott The First. Then a very odd coincidence occurred within a week of him dying.

George and Madge were out in their car and, if memory serves me correctly, had visited a rescue home in search of another Fox Terrier. They were unlucky and decided to return home and try somewhere else the next day. Then, while driving along a country road in the East Hyde area of Luton they spotted (yes, would you believe it!) a wire Fox Terrier wandering along the middle of the road. George stopped the car at once and spoke to the little dog, almost a replica of Bimbo Bott The First. They took him at once to the local police station where they were told they would have to wait for one week before they could claim him for their own.

During what must have been the longest week of George's and Madge's life they visited the police dog pound every day to check that he was still there. On the seventh day to their great joy he was given to them by the police, and his happy new life began with the Botts. He became known as Bimbo Bott The Second.

He stayed at my kennels every year for his fortnight holiday when George, Madge and another lady went off on holiday together. He was a placid little fellow for a wire Terrier, quiet and easy to handle.

It was about this time that I was involved with fund raising for PAWS and we had our first dog show, held at a nearby village hall. The Botts were delighted when Bimbo came second in the Terrier group and he posed proudly for the camera wearing his blue rosette.

He lived to be a good age. Sadly Madge died before him and he and George were left alone together. George moved away to Northampton to live with his sister but still used to bring Bimbo for his holidays. Then Bimbo died at a good age and George once again started looking for another companion.

**Nikki with Mr Bott**

I was able to point him in the direction of a breeder's kennels in the area that had a retired brood bitch needing a pet home. I spoke to Mrs S on the phone and she was glad for George to take the little Terrier. "Never a good idea to keep a wire boxed," she said, when we finalised the arrangements. So lucky little Nikki went to her new home with George, and once again I used to look after her.

I eventually had to give up my kennels, due to a new neighbour's objections, and changed to a cattery, so I gradually lost touch with George and his sister. He always sent me a Christmas card and in the last one I received he mentioned that Nikki had died, but he now had a Lakeland Terrier from the same kennels. Then the cards stopped coming and I assumed George had passed away and his sister was now the owner of the new Terrier.

## DUSTY

At the time of writing I now no longer board dogs. However I still have one canine friend who I care for every year when his owner, a retired professional tennis coach, living in Luton, goes to Wimbledon every July to act as steward for the two weeks.

Dusty was taken to the local vet surgery sixteen years ago with his other brothers and sisters, all of whom had been dumped as an unwanted litter.

Douglas Glenister had visited the surgery looking for a new dog and picked out Dusty a smooth coated black and tan German Shepherd x Labrador.

Dusty has been his devoted companion for over sixteen years. A lovely quiet dog, he has stayed with me every year from age twelve months. When I gave up my kennels I had not the heart to refuse Dusty after so much loyalty. So he still comes and stays in our house with our own three dogs. He is a dear boy, with a triangular-shaped face and an anxious eager to please expression.

He shares a close, almost psychic bond, with his owner and on the day when he is due to be collected starts to whine and become excited about one hour before Mr Glenister's car is heard on the drive. There is always a touching reunion and Dusty usually receives a gift on return: a souvenir Wimbledon tennis ball!

**Dusty**

## FRITZ

Our good friends Mike and Eileen Peters always owned Irish Setters. However they were left with Fritz a smooth coated Dachshund when Mike's elderly mother died some years ago. Fritz was quite old. I believe he was re-homed by me to Mrs Peters when his first owner had gone into a home. So the little dog was lucky to end his days with Mike and Eileen.

In spite of his small size and advanced years he had quite a presence. Oh yes, you couldn't ignore him and pretend he wasn't there! He had the typical hound's temperament, stubborn and single minded. He disappeared on a walk once while out with Mike and did not return home again for several hours. Obviously he was still not too old for a spot of hunting.

**Fritz**

I used to look after him when Mike and Eileen went on holiday and he always had to stay in the house due to the peculiar vocal way he had of expressing himself. He would pace continually when awake making a continuous UHUT, UHUT, UHUT! It went on and on without stopping, not particularly loud but just designed to irritate and jangle the nerves. " How much longer is he here for?" asked my long-suffering brother Anthony wearily one morning, as he left for work.

He'd just had a broken night's sleep punctuated by the noise of Fritz chugging round the house expressing himself in his usual inimitable style. I could never be angry with him; his long whipcord tail used to wag vigorously during his promenading and there was still a hint of mischief lurking in the depths of his sunken, faded eyes as he would look up at me with one fore paw raised. I could not bear to think of him being in a conventional boarding kennels behind bars peering out, uhut-ting away to himself until hoarse. So back he came, time after time to stay. The one good thing about him was that once he did lie down and go to sleep he would be out for the count in a deep slumber and wouldn't wake for hours. The trouble was it was always during the day, when the noise wouldn't have mattered; yes, Fritz was one of those awkward ones!

I don't know whether he carried on in the same way at home. Mike and Eileen never said. What I do know is, however, that after he died they reverted to their favourite breed, the Irish Setter!

## DOTTY (BOBO)

I really did some persuading for my friend of many years, Sue Hutchings, to agree to foster Dotty, an elderly Papillion left homeless when her owner passed away.

Sue had always owned Doberman Pinchers and at one time had kept four. She worked hard for animal welfare and was a keen fund raiser for different animal charities. Together we held jumble sales, coffee mornings and held three novelty dog shows.

Dotty, or Bobo as Sue named her, was at least sixteen when Sue took her in.

She looked after her devotedly for another two years. Trevor her husband, who had never before thought it possible he would become so fond of such a tiny scrap like Dotty, after the Doberman collection, was very upset when she died.

Like poor little Billy the Yorkie, she had a tremendous fighting spirit and zest for life.

I know Sue and Trevor still miss her.

**Dotty**

# BESIDES THE BYES

*If there's a canine Paradise it must be Sidmouth in the Byes*
*Where dogs all take their owners for their daily exercise.*

## PICKLES AND NICKY

I could not write this book about rescued pets without mentioning Pickles, a spotted brown and white Jack Russell terrier, and Nicky, yet another wire Fox Terrier who belongs to our friends Vera King and Pat Guthrie, who both sometimes stay with us in Sidmouth.

**Pickles and Nicky with Vera and Pat**

Pickles is the second Jack Russell Vera has owned; her first was another rescue from PAWS, called Sammy, who lived with Vera for twelve years. I saw an advertisement for Pickles in the local pet shop after Sammy had died. Pickles was looking for a home because the family who owned him had two other larger dogs and were finding it expensive to look after three. He was left shut in all day while the family was out. Vera made the journey from Croydon to see him and brought him home with her. He is a dear, happy little chap and loves his yearly Sidmouth holidays. Vera is a retired actress, and you can often hear her rich, booming stage-trained voice fluting through the Byes when Pickles has disappeared after a rabbit!

Pat Guthrie has always up until now owned Airedales. Alec, her late husband, and Pat have been good friends of ours for over twenty years. Ruff, their much loved Airedale, was mated to our Airedale, Nan, in 1987 and they had ten puppies. So we go a long way back.

Pat now wanted a smaller dog after Alec and Ted (Ruff's son) had died. I heard about Nicky, another retired stud Fox Terrier from the same kennels from which George Bott's dog, Nikki, had been bred. My brother drove Pat over to look at him. A perfect little gentleman he proved to be, very much like our first wire, Asta, of many years back.

His only fault is that he will escape if given the chance. Poor Pat has had several anxious moments when he has disappeared from her garden. Once she paid out a substantial sum to two lucky schoolboys - who found him and brought him home after one of his days out. He often stays with us when Pat goes away, and he always arrives in a taxi with more luggage to unload than his mistress.

# PAW PRINTS

## MY GOD IS A DOUBLE DEITY

### A Twenty-Third Psalm according to Chloé, the Rescued Boxer

My God is a couple, I shall not want.
They allow me to lie down on soft carpets.
They lead me beside the playful Sid.

They restore my soul:
They lead me in the paths of pleasure
For their names' sake.

Yea, though I scamper
Through the Byes, which could be
The valley of the shadow of death,
I shall fear no pitt bull terrier
For You are with me:
Your bag and my leash
They comfort me.

You prepare a huge bowl before me
In the presence of jealous felines;
You fondle my head with kind digits.
My water bowl is always brimming.

Surely goodness and mercy shall
Follow me all the days of my life
And I shall dwell in the Sidmouth home
Of my Gods for ever.

Copyright © Anne Everest-Phillips 2004

(with acknowledgements to King David, the Psalmist)

**Chloé with Anne and Roger**

## White

My little dog stands out
Against the dark and shade,
A West Highland White Terrier,
That's how she's made.
White pointed ears,
White upright tail,
White teeth.
Pink tongue, pink skin
Beneath white fur,
If you could but see that's her.
Black button nose and eyes
Black pads beneath white paws
And some black claws.
But that's alright
For all the rest of her is white.

**© Stewart Gordon**

**Topsy**

**Tamar**

## Ice of night

chilling
toes
so move closer
to the dog
plumping
cushions into back
tuck
feet under sleeping
fur
nestle deep
soft
warm and sweet
comforting
as new-baked bread.

**© Juliette Woodward**
February 2005

# TITBITS

**SAM**

*If you think a wader is a water bird
then it's obvious you haven't heard
of Sam and co.
Sam is apt quite frequently to go
into the pond. Not for a swim,
that would be too dull for him,
but steeplechasing through the weeds for a duck or two
or, preferably three.*

*The ducks do not care to be
components of Sam's next High Tea
so hurry off, start circulating.*

*Sam finds this intoxicating.
With crash and splash he makes a dash -
the ducks do too. All are now gyrating.*

*Sam's owner tries to catch his eye, his ear,
his mind, his stumpy tail.
she gives a call, a shriek, her full vocabulary -
all to no avail.*

*He doesn't hear at all.
Sam and the pond are small, so he
needs all his concentration
for rapid circumnavigation.*

*His owner, in great haste,
wades in water to her waist.
It's not a suicide you
see as you go by
the apple tree, but Sam's owner hanging out to dry.*

### EMMA

*Her mission is to heal.*
*She knows when you have toothache,*
*licks with urgent zeal.*

*Emma will be there to give*
*as long as ye both live*

**© P D Pemberton**

### BESSIE

*My newly-rescued dog is*
*entirely delightful.*
*She's not afraid of people,*
*loves meeting them;*
*but finds high-pitched ranting*
*politicians on TV*
*entirely frightful*

**© P D Pemberton**

# TALES END

*Serenely she regards us with a non-judgmental eye*
*She has no rule of paw to measure human error by.*
*Trusting, loyal and constantly*
*At our side, quick to defend,*
*Faith our Airedale terrier*
*Always and ever our best friend.*

2004 was not a happy year for us as far as family pets were concerned. In May we had to have our rescue Siamese cat, Kang, put to sleep due to kidney failure. He was a great character and much missed by Anthony my brother and myself. Then in December our senior statesman cat, the dignified Willoughby, a strong old tabby, died from a pulmonary thrombosis. Both cats were unwanted and had lived with us for several years and were happy.

But the most devastating blow happened in June when we lost our funny little Airedale Terrier, Faith, to a bone tumour in her hind leg. She was aged only 6, cut down in her prime. We had never lost a dog so young before, all of the others had lived beyond 13, with Nan, the great matriarch of the canine family, reaching 16 and a half, after mothering twenty-three puppies.

Losing sensitive, clumsy, loyal little Faith with her funny little sideways pointing right ear broke our hearts. It's bad enough to lose an old pet - it is to be expected as the year pass - but six was nothing, it was so unfair.

For one week we were without an Airedale in the house. It was the first time for twenty years. Little Guy, our wire haired Terrier who had grown up with Faith, (they were two naughty partners in crime together for six years) missed her dreadfully.

I made about thirty phone calls to breeders all over the country but there were no rescued bitches available. We decided we did not want a puppy at this stage. At last I was lucky - a lady I rang had heard of somebody who knew somebody … who had a seven-year-old retired brood bitch called Cassie who needed a home.

The following Sunday after Faith died (in between us, on the back lawn, on the previous Saturday), we made the journey up the M1 to a breeders' kennels thirty miles from Doncaster. We had Guy, and Gemma our 15-year-old Yorkie, with us. After all, they had to approve of the prospective newcomer too.

The couple who owned the kennels took us round to the exercise paddock and let Cassie out. A very fit and feisty-looking Airedale bounded straight past us without so much as a look in our direction, and disappeared into the bushes to investigate. I felt a vague disappointment. She was not really what we'd expected, although of course we couldn't expect a replica Faith. On the breeders' advice we walked Cassie, Guy and Gemma up the lane together, Cassie ploughed along with her nose to the ground ignoring everyone, other dogs included, intent only on scents and getting out of her kennel.

When we got back we asked the breeders if they thought she would be all right with Guy and Gemma. They were honest with us when they told us that although she would never start a fight she would easily finish one if she was provoked. That decided us: Guy could easily provoke!

I asked if they had any more. Well, there was Tess; she was 4 and had been bred for showing, but after being knocked by a car as a young pup, was left as a companion kennel mate to her mother, who had died last year. She wouldn't have to be exercised far though because of that damaged pelvis.

So at our request she was brought out for our inspection. An altogether different little girl trotted demurely out from the kennel, came straight up to us and started to wiggle and waggle her entire body. We noticed her tail hung like a lamb's behind her, no doubt the legacy of the early accident.

Yes, this was more like it, not exactly like Faith of course but very similar. She and Guy bonded well. Gemma ignored her which was OK, and home she came with us. I do hope Cassie found a good home - I'm sure she did eventually.

Tess appeared to be rather hungry and happily devoured a pork pie and several little cakes on the three-hour-journey home. "Don't spoil and pamper her!" the down-to-earth breeder from Doncaster advised us, with a knowing twinkle in his eye, as we left "We up north know what you southerners are like with dogs, you are too soft!"

**Guy and Faith**

**Gemma with Faith**

**Hetty**

Yes, maybe he was right, but you can't change the habits of a lifetime. We knew she was the dog for us and, as Anthony said, she'd had a poor start in life - a nasty accident when so young, and probably missing her mother, and always being kept in a kennel.

She settled in happily. We changed her name to Hetty; it seemed to suit her. It was a name from the twenties' and thirties' era, when Airedales were at the peak of their popularity. Many homes kept one as a pet, and they were used for police work and by the armed forces as messenger dogs.

Today Hetty's tail is perpendicular and is carried with characteristic Airedale jauntiness. Her life of boredom in a kennel environment is now thankfully past history.

I can see Faith's eagerness to please in her, and also she has the same kindly wisdom of Nan from many years past. We also recognize feisty, independent Grace, Nan's daughter, in the newcomer Hetty - "I wouldn't mind being left on my own if you don't mind!"

We hoped her good behaviour when she arrived would rub off on to Guy but of course it hasn't. The reverse has happened and now the two are always working in tandem trouble together. But that's Terriers - we have owned them for almost thirty years and love their high spirits and naughtiness. We wouldn't have owned so many if we'd found them too much of a challenge.

And after all life would be very dull without a challenge!

# ACKNOWLEDGEMENTS

I should like to thank the following for their generous support of Wag Tales:

**MAIN SPONSOR**: Axel Dubois of Royal Canin

Also the following companies, organizations, and individuals, in alphabetical order:

| | |
|---|---|
| AJM PRODUCTS (Penny Adair) | THE KENNELS AGENCY |
| ANIMAL AUNTS (Gillie McNicholl) | Lealands Women's Club, Luton |
| BAYER ANIMAL HEALTH (Karrie Day) | Andy and Min Milton |
| BARKING MAD (Lea Southern) | Gwen Porteous |
| Frida Harris | Limbury WI, Bedfordshire |
| A J Hill | Silsoe WI, Bedfordshire |
| HILL'S PET NUTRITION | Tingrith WI, Bedfordshire |
| JOHNSON'S PET PRODUCTS | Toddington WI, Bedfordshire |
| KENNEL NUTRITION LTD | WAGG FOODS |

I should also like to thank:

Margot Collingbourn-Beevers of d'Arblays Press for her advice and help with the painstaking task of editing and preparing Wag Tales for publication;

Anthony Fensom for support and encouragement, and practical work on the computer;

Paul Betts for editing some of the photographs;

The Hon Tania Coleridge for writing the Foreword;

and Vikki Tarr of ARCHANT SOUTH WEST PUBLICATIONS.

Thank you also to all pet owners who contributed their stories and photographs, and to the dogs themselves – without whom there would not have been any Wag Tales to tell!

# AFTERWORD

For the elderly housebound person living alone, a pet is often vital to health and well-being. When such a person becomes ill and has to go into hospital, or into a permanent residential home, a choice has to be faced in deciding what will become of the companion, animal, or bird.

It is here that the Cinnamon Trust provides an invaluable service by offering either temporary or permanent foster homes for pets of owners who have become too ill to look after their beloved companions.

It is a unique charity in that the animals are cared for in a volunteer's own home, or at one of two sanctuaries based in Cornwall and Devon. The two sanctuaries cater mostly for quite elderly pets, or for those with special needs. This home-from-home transition is much less stressful for the pet concerned than being suddenly uprooted, probably for the first time in its life, and installed in a strange environment such as a boarding cattery or kennels, however well managed and maintained. The owner of the pet will also have peace of mind, knowing that the faithful companion(s) has found an ideal home environment, on either a temporary or permanent basis.

I hope people will buy Wag Tales, the profits from which will go to the Cinnamon Trust. Also, I am sure that the people who have contributed the stories of their own rescued dogs will be proud to know that they have played a part in helping both the pets, and their owners, from the sales of this book.

**Jenny Fensom**
May 2005

## THE CINNAMON TRUST

10 Market Square, Hayle, Cornwall TR27 4HE

*Tel*: 01736 757900

*Fax*: 01736 757010

*email*: admin@cinnamon.org.uk